# WHAT OTHERS SAY ABOUT
## *RESTORING YOUR HEART TO DEEPEN INTIMACY*

*Real. Transparent. Transforming.* These are just a few of the words that
linger in my heart and mind as I walk away from the personal encounter
I had with God through reading this book. In it, Norma Donovan shares
her healing journey and her desire to connect deeper with the Lover
of our souls, and her passion for each of us to experience this same
redemptive and freeing work is undeniable and inviting. As a Christian
counselor, I not only felt drawn to engage in my own personal journey,
but I also had many clients come to mind who would benefit from the
well-developed concepts, truths, and practical steps offered to guide and
propel one into emotional healing and freedom. *Restoring Your Heart
to Deepen Intimacy* will prove to be a unique resource that perpetually
invites each reader to launch into a progressive, transformative journey. Plan for your reading experience to be a "marker" along the way to
living life as God intended — being fully loved and walking with Him in
wholeness and freedom.

— JO LYNN BRIGHT, LCMFT, CST,
LICENSED CLINICAL MARRIAGE AND FAMILY THERAPIST
AND CERTIFIED CHRISTIAN SEX THERAPIST

In my opinion, the best books come out of the crucible of real-life
experience. That's why I wholeheartedly recommend *Restoring Your
Heart to Deepen Intimacy*, written by my sister, friend, and co-laborer in
the gospel. I believe that Norma Donovan has been empowered to pen a
"kingdom emancipation" of the heart because she herself has been freed
by the Lover of her soul. May this book supernaturally find its way into
the hands of the broken and chained, so that they too may enter into the
Father's healing embrace.

— SAM MCVAY, FOUNDER OF DISCIPLE NATIONS

If you are looking for a means to privately ignite a spiritual journey of renewal, this book is for you. Norma Donovan's step-by-step guidance and journaling prompts probe deeper into the heart of the matter between you and God. Her human, transparent, and sometimes humorous experiences also endear her to you and illustrate practical ways to discover your identity in Christ while building hope. Norma uncovers God's truth and commitment to you while exposing the handicaps of self-rejection and shame; she invites you to reflect and journal, giving you the opportunity to shut the door on fear, identify villains of condemnation, and ward off the distractions keeping you from deeper intimacy with God; and she slowly ignites within you a hunger for God's peace and presence, replacing even a dying flame with a hunger for deeper intimacy. More than a good read, *Restoring Your Heart to Deepen Intimacy* engages you to live and rest as his beloved.

— CHARITY SCHAULIS, PROFESSIONAL COACH
AND TRAINER, CERTIFIED BY THE INTERNATIONAL
COACHING FEDERATION WWW.CHARITYSCHAULIS.COM

Norma Donovan is a wounded healer. She has taken her knowledge as a mentor and author, along with her fifty years of walking with the Lord, to produce a masterpiece, integrating psychological principles with spiritual truths. This is an exceedingly practical work, with moments of reflection built in. It is an invitation to dig deep, to uncover the wounds that block us from intimacy with God, and to allow our heavenly Father to heal us.

— JENNIFER CECIL, MED LPC, LICENSED PROFESSIONAL
COUNSELOR, CHRISTIAN COUNSELING SERVICES

So many of us struggle with the bondage of shame, guilt, and discouragement. Norma Donovan takes us deeper into how Jesus can set us on the road to freedom. Norma's heart to help us unwrap our many hurts is heard throughout *Restoring Your Heart to Deepen Intimacy*. I highly recommend this book for Bible studies, church recovery programs, and any group looking for deeper intimacy with Christ.

— JULIE A. SHRADER, FOUNDER AND CHIEF
EXECUTIVE OFFICER, REJUVENATING WOMEN
AND THE RESTORED WINGS PROGRAM

While reading Norma Donovan's *Restoring Your Heart to Deepen Intimacy*, I asked the Father to show me any open doors that may have allowed unknown strongholds into my own life. God, in His perfect and completing grace, reached into the moments I spent in these pages, and He set my heart free from chains that were long forgotten but still affected me and those I love. It is in this context that I encourage you to take time to allow God to use this powerful book to gently, kindly, and forever set you free from the bondage that may still be holding you captive. Don't rush through; whether you are a young follower of Christ or have been on this journey for a long time, you will be blessed as this work leads you to linger with the Father. I believe you are about to embark on what will become one of the greatest spiritual adventures of your life and that God will meet you right where you are. There, in the vulnerable, tender places of your soul, He will speak peace and leave beauty in exchange for your ashes.

— CATHY TURNER, ASSOCIATE PASTOR OF CHRIST
CHURCH, FOUNDER OF HOPE RANCH FOR WOMEN

In *Restoring Your Heart to Deepen Intimacy*, Norma Donovan weaves together a tapestry of her personal journey and guiding principles of truth to challenge us to pursue God more deeply.

— PAUL WHITE, PHD, PSYCHOLOGIST AND
COAUTHOR OF THE BESTSELLING *THE 5 LANGUAGES
OF APPRECIATION IN THE WORKPLACE*

# RESTORING YOUR HEART TO DEEPEN INTIMACY

*Finding Wholehearted Devotion to God Through Emotional Healing*

## Norma Donovan

*To Steve and Mindy Peterson. Thank you for your faithful investment in my emotional healing. You loved and accepted me despite all of my hurt. Many captives have been set free because of your devotion to give wise counsel and instruction from God's truth.*

"Then you will know the truth, and
the truth will set you free."

JOHN 8:32

# CONTENTS

# PREFACE

ONCE YOU EXPERIENCE FREEDOM, you want others to experience it too. In my case, I experienced emotional freedom, and I want others to experience the same.

Emotional freedom cannot come, however, unless there is, first, emotional healing. For me, this healing happened over time and through various methods. Studying Scripture, praying, and declaring prophetic words were all a large part of my emotional healing process. I received insight from Christian lay counselors at church as well as professional counselors. In college, I went on to study my master's degree in counseling and quickly gained interest in analyzing myself and others. Emotional healing and intimacy with God thus became my two passions (which you could easily discern by looking at the books I've collected on my shelves over the years!).

Much of my healing, though, came from reading Christian books on emotional hurt and wholeness and allowing the Grand Counselor, the Holy Spirit, to give me "revelation truth" that set me free. In particular, I learned from Thom Gardner's book, *Healing the Wounded Heart*, how to see my memories differently through God's truth. Thom Gardner writes, "Once the Lord has taken us to a root memory where the lie is contained, we simply ask Him to reveal to us His presence and the truth regarding the situation in the memory..." Through prayer and by faith, I used Gardner's method, asking the Holy Spirit to show me a specific memory by which a negative emotion, such as fear, had come into my life. When a memory came to me, I journaled about what I had seen and felt at the time, and the lies that I had come to believe. Next, I invited the Lord into my memory. I listened to what He said, observed His character and actions, and allowed Him to comfort me, all within that memory. I was amazed at how inviting Jesus into my painful scenarios made all the difference in my emotional healing. Each time I reframed my memory with His truth, the lies I believed were revealed and refuted, and I received a little more emotional wholeness.

Then early in 1991, my pastor prophesied over me that I would "heal hearts." In his mind, he believed this would be in regard to physical healing, but as I recounted his prophetic word to a friend, the Holy Spirit revealed that He would use me as His conduit to bring emotional healing — the healing of hearts.

Twenty years later, in 2011, a young friend fortified this prophecy with another word: "God has given you *many* personal testimonies, which attest to His goodness and the power of His redeeming love and heart of restoration!"

This combination of factors — my journey through emotional hurt, restoration, freedom, and intimacy; the passion that God has given me for these topics; and my desire to obey God's assignment to use my personal testimony to heal hearts — is what motivated the writing of this book.

As such, *Restoring Your Heart to Deepen Intimacy* mostly testifies to God's goodness, redeeming love, and heart for restoration, but it also provides a glimpse of my emotional healing journey. Because others' stories sometimes help us see our own lives more clearly, I pray the Holy Spirit will use my anecdotes and the lessons I've learned from them as a way to bring restoration and freedom through the back door of your heart. After all, this is a book of promises from the Word of God that I have mined and applied to my life, and these same promises are yours.

My desire is that, in reading this book, you will not only encounter emotional healing but, as a result of your newfound wholeness, will draw closer to God and those you love. Of course, emotional wholeness and intimacy with God will never be fully attained this side of heaven; for me, the process has taken more than twenty years, and I'm still learning! But progress *is* possible. So won't you join me on the journey?

# INTRODUCTION:
# EMOTIONAL
# HEART ATTACKS

*When Jesus saw him lying there and learned that*
*he had been in this condition for a long time,*
*he asked him, "Do you want to get well?"*

JOHN 5:6

Friday, June 4, 2010. Late afternoon.

I experienced what I thought was heartburn while chatting on the phone with a young friend. We were discussing the logistics of our next morning's bike ride, as we were training for an upcoming triathlon. Thirty minutes later my physician-husband and I sat down to dinner. I picked at the food on my plate, and John asked, "What's wrong?"

"I think I have indigestion."

"Take some antacids," he suggested.

I chewed some antacids and got ready to attend a church meeting that evening. A prophetic speaker from Scotland would be the guest speaker. Despite the uncomfortable pressure in my chest, I decided to attend. Midway through worship, I felt as if I had the flu, so I sat down.

As my head hit the pillow that night, the pain in my chest seemed to radiate toward my back. John wanted us to go to the emergency room, but I wanted to sleep. After all, a good night's sleep would surely bring refreshment for our early-morning bike ride with friends.

During the night, my chest pain went away. We woke up to the gentle *pitter-pat* of rain against the windowsill, which postponed our bike ride. John decided to go into work.

Pondering how I'd felt the night before, curiosity led me to the computer. I googled "female heart attack symptoms." One of the first symptoms that came up was denial. *I'd better call the doctor.* The doctor on call discouraged me from going on our bike ride until I'd had an EKG to make sure my heart checked out okay. I called John, and he immediately came home to take me to the emergency room.

"I think I had a heart attack last night," brought immediate attention from four ER nurses. The results of a few tests revealed that I'd had a mild heart attack, most likely caused by a stress-induced spasm. A cardiac catheterization the next day revealed no blockage.

"You might not have awakened," the doctor said. He reprimanded me for going to sleep the night before with my symptoms. I am fortunate and grateful my heart attack didn't have any life-threatening effects. But the scenario gave John and I a renewed gratefulness for what mattered most: faith, family, and friends.

It also made me realize that, just as clogged coronary arteries prevent us from living life to the fullest, so do unhealthy emotional hearts. While a blocked heart artery makes it difficult to physically exert ourselves, unforgiveness and other emotional blockages lodged deep within our hearts can make it difficult to be close to people and to God. Said more simply, woundedness restricts our emotional and spiritual growth.

## Who Is This Book For?

None of us goes through life without getting wounded or broken. In that sense, this book can benefit just about anyone! However, as with any book, some readers will benefit more than others. Take some time and prayerfully respond to these questions:

- Do you struggle with rejection, shame, or discouragement?
- Are you tired of hiding behind the performance mask, wishing you could be yourself, but you don't even know who that person is?
- Do you want to no longer be held captive by fear so that you can fulfill your God-given destiny?
- Do you desire to extend God's gift of grace to yourself and to those you meet?
- When you are emotionally "bumped," like a hot button being pushed, is there a side of yourself you wish didn't exist?

If you answered yes to any of these questions, this book is especially for you.

In addition, although this book is written from a woman's perspective, I believe it can benefit men and women equally, as we all have experienced abandonment, rejection, shame, fear, and believing lies. God created both women and men with an appetite for becoming intimate with Him and with others. Intimacy with God is for everyone!

## What Is Emotional Restoration?

I believe that when God first breathes life into our souls, when we are still inside our mothers' wombs, our hearts are whole. That is, they are unbroken, unhurt, and unimpaired. Said another way, they are healthy, well, and complete. As we make our way further into this broken world, however, things such as hurt, offense, and loss inevitably come into play, and our hearts become broken, wounded, and incomplete. The good news is that God, the Maker of our hearts, can heal and restore our hearts back to their original states, making them whole again. And when He does, we gain the freedom to be who He created us to be, no longer needing to hide behind defenses or to cope in unhealthy ways.

As you read through this book, you will see me describe these concepts using the terms below. While I often use these terms interchangeably, I think it's important to note the subtle differences between them.

- **Emotional wholeness** — the original state of our God-created hearts, which is unbroken, unhurt, and unimpaired (or healthy, well, and complete).

- **Emotional hurt and healing** — *hurt* is the pain and brokenness that enters our hearts as the inevitable result of living in a fallen world, while *healing* is the process of binding, or mending, our broken hearts, restoring them to health and wellness. Just as physical bodies need healing when they are sick or broken, so too do emotional hearts when they are hurt, broken, wounded, or ill.

- **Emotional restoration** — similar to emotional healing, this is the process of restoring an incomplete heart back to its original state of wholeness. God creates our hearts to be whole, and only by way of hurt, offense, and loss do they become unwhole. (I also refer to this as *heart restoration.*)

- **Emotional freedom** — the result of emotional healing and restoration. Having emotional freedom means being free to be who God created us to be, no longer needing to hide behind defenses or to cope in unhealthy ways.

## How Is This Book Like a Mediterranean Cruise?

*Restoring Your Heart to Deepen Intimacy* is divided into two parts. The first part, "Restoring Your Heart," pertains to emotional restoration. The chapters start by recounting my personal experiences with emotional hurt, tackling the issues of abandonment and an absent father and looking at the processes of forgiveness and establishing healthy attachment to God. Each chapter covers a particular hurtful memory that God revealed to me as I used Thom Gardner's method of seeing memories differently through God's truth (detailed in the preface). Each chapter then ends with the same hurtful memory, now reframed in the presence of God. Through these stories, we'll discover together how to embrace God's grace in place of shame and His unconditional acceptance in place of rejection. We'll also learn how to renew our minds with God's truth instead of believing the enemy's lies, while exchanging our fear and anxiety with faith and peace.

The second half of the book, "Deepening Intimacy," is about how to develop and deepen our intimacy with God. We will see how knowing, loving, and obeying God is a cycle: as we get to know God, we can't help but love Him, which, in turn, causes us to obey Him. We will also see how learning who God is can lead us to discover our identity — who we are and who He has created us to be. Then in the final two chapters, we will reflect on two spiritual disciplines that have brought me personally closer to God: actively seeking to be in His presence and to hear His voice.

You might think of this book as being similar to a Mediterranean cruise, in that I will visit numerous "countries," or cover many topics, but my stay at each place or concept will be brief. The difference, in this case, is that I encourage you to regularly get off the cruise ship to make your own personal observations. Sprinkled throughout each chapter, you will find hearts turned on their sides, which you can interpret as a nudge to do so. Each of these hearts precedes a question to ponder to help you through your own journey of heart restoration. So when you see this symbol:

take a breath, review what you just read, chew on it, and ask the Holy Spirit how it applies to your life. Like the word "Selah" in the book of Psalms, these hearts are a signal for you to pause and reflect on what you just read.

At the end of every chapter are two sections: "What I Heard My Father Say" is a prophetic word for you to receive as your own. I pray that these sections reveal the Father's heart for you and minister encouragement and hope. "The Heart of the Matter" then rounds up each chapter, reviewing the main concepts that you can take away and, if needed, revisit later.

## The Thing about Freedom

Often there is a cost to freedom; emotional freedom is no different.

The first cost, and the first step, to achieving freedom of any kind is awareness of what is holding you captive. Becoming aware of the pain that enslaves you is often uncomfortable at first, but it is necessary in order to know what you need to be free from. As such, I hope God uses *Restoring Your Heart to Deepen Intimacy* as a tool to help you become aware of your unhealed and unredeemed hurts and recognize how they have prevented you from true intimacy, so that you can clear the path to emotional healing and restoration.

Second, emotional freedom requires vulnerability — opening up our hearts in order to remove the hurt. In the same way that heart attacks are caused by a buildup of cholesterol or plaque inside the arteries, which choke off the blood supply to the heart, undealt-with hurt, disappointment, and unforgiveness can build up and block a person's emotional heart from receiving what it needs. Our typical reaction to being hurt is to hide and self-protect, which only causes our brokenness and hurt to build up and keeps our heart in a weakened state. We can prevent and reverse this buildup and strengthen our heart by being vulnerable with a trusted confidant, with God, or even just with yourself. We must open up our hearts.

Finally, freedom requires time and intention. As Katherine Reay wrote in *Dear Mr. Knightley*, "Changing, being real and becoming who you want to be, is hard work." So, too, is the emotional healing process. Information alone doesn't always bring change; it's the revelation and application of that information that brings heart transformation. Therefore, I recommend having a journal next to you while you read this book, so that you can respond to questions and jot down any notable thoughts and emotions you have along the way. Take your time and slowly process your life through the principles offered. In prayer, beseech the Holy Spirit, your counselor, to lead you to activate your own healing journey. And should you need further help, please reach out to a Christian counselor.

I applaud you for picking up this book. Reading *Restoring Your Heart to Deepen Intimacy* is an investment in your emotional health and wholeness, which is an investment in your intimacy with God and others. The artwork on the front cover, titled "Brave Heart," aptly describes your courageousness to tackle your emotional well-being.

## "Do You Want to Get Well?"

Chapter five of the Gospel of John tells the story of a man who was an invalid for thirty-eight years. He and several others were lying by the Bethesda pool, waiting for the moving of the waters. Every now and then, an angel of the Lord would come down and stir the waters. One person got into the pool and was healed of disease. "When Jesus saw him lying there and learned that he had been in this condition for a long time, He asked him, 'Do you want to get well?'"[1]

The Lord is asking us the same question today. Emotional wholeness is our decision and responsibility. Many of us, like the disabled person in the verse above, have been emotionally impaired for a long time. Some people stay in the comfort of their emotional hurts and wounds, because anything else feels too scary and uncomfortable. But we have a choice — we can stay by the pool of Bethesda and remain an emotional invalid or embrace emotional freedom and take up our mat and walk.

If you want to be made well, keep reading. The waters are being stirred, and the Holy Spirit is by your side. Let the Spirit of God pick you up and place you in the pool. It's not by coincidence you have this book. I believe God is directing your steps, and He's inviting you into deeper intimacy with Him through emotional restoration. This is your time, your moment for decision and action, for having your heart restored and your intimacy with God and others deepened.

# PART 1: RESTORING YOUR HEART

Abandonment, rejection, shame, fear. Most of us have experienced one or more of these types of emotional hurts in our lifetime. In the first half of this book, chapters 1 through 4, you'll discover where these specific types of hurts commonly originate, how they can negatively impact your life and relationships, and how you can begin to clear them out of your heart. Chapter 5 then shows you how to identify and uproot your belief in the lies that led to those hurts and to replace them with attachment and acceptance, and God's grace, faith, peace, and truth.

My prayer for each of you as you navigate through these chapters comes from Isaiah 61:1: "The Spirit of the Sovereign Lord is on me, because the Lord has anointed me to preach good news to the poor. He has sent me to bind up the brokenhearted, to proclaim freedom for the captives and release from darkness for the prisoners." May Jesus heal your broken heart, set you free, and release you into the light of His truth. And may you experience the emotional healing that will help you to grow closer to others and, especially, to God.

# — 1 —
# ATTACHED

*I will be a Father to you, and you will be my
sons and daughters, says the Lord Almighty.*

2 CORINTHIANS 6:18

"Norma, Dad may not walk you down the aisle tomorrow." Like a dropped bomb, those devastating words from Mom's mouth during my wedding rehearsal caused my world to crash around me. I sat on the pew and began to weep.

Most little girls dream about their wedding day. I know I did, and I wanted the first most-important man in my life to be there to celebrate. I couldn't believe that my uncle might be the one who would give me away to my beloved John.

For reasons unknown, even to my precious dad, he was having a hard time letting go of his "baby" daughter. Dad did end up walking me down the aisle, but he did not come to the rehearsal dinner at the Arizona Country Club or attend the wedding reception held in my parents' backyard.

Now, over forty years later, I can still see my dad driving in the opposite direction as John and I headed to the reception. Shame filled my heart, and rejection permeated my thoughts. I felt abandoned by my dad on my special day.

Two things saved me that weekend of May 22, 1976. First, John and I knew Dad approved of our relationship and had blessed our marriage. The beauty of repression acted as a second protective covering, allowing me to enjoy the festivities of that day regardless. And for many years after that, I suppressed the hurt, as it confirmed what I already believed: *I am unlovable and unacceptable.* I don't recommend stuffing emotions. However, when it's just too hurtful, God allows it until we can sift through it later.

Ten years after we married, the initial signs of my father-wound began to surface like an iceberg poking its head up from the surface. I made the judgment, "Men aren't there for me at significant times in my life." I didn't realize at the time that Dad's absence at my wedding festivities had caused me to formulate that judgment. In fact, I didn't realize that I even believed that lie until it looked as if my husband might not be at our son's birth. John, a urologic resident, called to say that he had numerous surgical cases the week of our son's due date and that if we wanted him to be at the delivery, we would need to have David induced ten days early. I called Mom and cried hysterically over the phone. My overreaction to John's suggestion hinted to me that I had an unhealed hurt, but I wasn't aware of what that hurt was. I later recognized the unconscious judgment I had made about men and realized that this judgment had made me afraid that John, like my dad, would abandon me at this important time in our lives. Fortunately, however, John was present to see our son born.

Then nearly two decades after the day of our wedding, the painful memory began to emerge like an iceberg making its entrance from under the depths of the ocean, leaving me with emotional holes. My heart, now like a sieve, allowed various hurts from my past to seep through.

Fortunately, God, in His sovereignty, has an amazing way of turning the worst moments into the greatest opportunities for His glory. He takes the "yuck" in our lives and redeems it for our good. In my case, He did this through the church's counseling ministry, which helped me to recognize that I had formed misconceptions about God as my Father, caused by the hurt, rejection, and shame I felt from my biological dad. Once I realized that, I was able to dive straight into the arms of my loving, heavenly Father. I became intentional in having time alone with God. And through prayer, reading God's Word, sitting still, and listening to His voice, I grew in my understanding of God's love for me.

## Father God Misconceptions

*As a father has compassion on his children, so the*
*Lord has compassion on those who fear him.*

PSALM 103:13

Many little girls grow up desiring to be affectionately known as "Daddy's Girl," and I certainly was no different. I longed to be that special little girl in my daddy's eyes. I wanted to feel my papa's delight and adoration. I wanted not only to feel Dad's love but to know that he liked me enough to spend time with me.

Dads shape their children's lives. The way fathers treat their children and the things they give or withhold from them can affect both girls' and boys' expectations of men and male authority. As a result, whether we realize it or not, fathers play a key role in the ability of men and women to trust God. Dads are our first impression of male authority, and it's easy to transfer how we feel or what we believe about our earthly fathers onto God the Father.

If you hold a negative view of God, it may stem from your relationship with your earthly father. You may have had a dad who was not there for you, or one who was harsh and critical, and you may have projected that onto your heavenly Dad. Further, inaccurately assessing God will have a negative effect on how you view yourself.

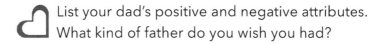 List your dad's positive and negative attributes. What kind of father do you wish you had?

My dad was a distant father — physically present but emotionally absent. As a result, I lacked bonding or attachment to him. Even though my dad was affectionate and told me he loved me, we had little emotional connection.

Dad was also an alcoholic, which meant things were unpredictable. I never knew what kind of mood he'd be in. He would get angry and, at times, violently punch holes in a wall or door. Though I experienced no physical abuse, I did not always feel safe with him.

Fueling my feelings of rejection, Dad would make critical statements toward me, and he neglected spending time alone with me. Never feeling "good enough," I always tried to please him. Any Daddy-daughter times we did have were spent shopping at an army-surplus store or going to a swap meet, doing things he wanted to do. It was not until I was twenty-four and had my master's degree in counseling that Dad told me, "I'm proud of you."

But through this, I learned a valuable life truth: you can't give away what you don't possess. If you asked to borrow a million dollars from me, for example, I couldn't give it to you, simply because I don't possess it. In other words, I believe that when my dad was a child, he didn't receive the love he desperately needed — so when he grew up, he could not give me the love I needed. Even if he had wanted to make me feel like a daddy's girl, he couldn't have, because his own unhealed emotional wounds prevented him.

Living in the environment I did encouraged me to become a codependent, peace-at-any-price person. As a child, I walked on eggshells at home, as I didn't want to rock the boat. I also became a people pleaser, in general, and a "Miss Goody Two Shoes." Shame and low self-worth caused me to hide behind various masks, fearful that the real me would be rejected.

Because of this experience with my dad, I came to believe that God the Father was also distant and not there for me. My inaccurate perceptions of God, in turn, caused me to fear Him in an unhealthy way: I considered Him unapproachable and unpredictable, and I thought I couldn't count on Him. I believed that my heavenly Father didn't want to connect with me and that He, too, had rejected me.

How has your relationship with your earthly dad affected your perceptions of God the Father and your ability to trust Him?

## The Role of Attachment

*Never will I leave you; never will I forsake you.*

HEBREWS 13:5

I lacked *attachment*, or a strong bond, with my earthly dad. However, God created each of us to experience a healthy attachment to both Him and others. Christian psychologist Dr. Henry Cloud, in *Changes that Heal,* says, "Without relationship, without attachment to God and others, we can't be our true selves."

### The Three Characteristics of Attachment Behavior

It's in our attachment to our heavenly Father, our caregiver, where our security lies. In the study of psychology, attachment theory says that for children to feel secure, their caregivers must display the following three attachment behaviors: they must be **present**, **attentive**, and **responsive**. Our heavenly Daddy is all three of these things and more.

First of all, God is always **present.** He promises each of us in Hebrews 13:5 that He will never leave or abandon us. God will never give up on us or turn His back on us when we sin. He'll never say, "That's it! You've crossed the line. I'm going to disown you!" God's very name Immanuel means "God with us." Sometimes, for several reasons, we may not feel God is near, but the truth remains He is.

Having a caregiver who is not present causes feelings of abandonment and a lack of security. In fact, I can trace most of my fears back to the root fear of abandonment: my earthly dad was physically present but emotionally distant, he provided for my daily needs but wasn't actively engaged or involved in my life, and my passions were not a priority to him (for example, he rarely attended our high school musical performances). It wasn't until I was in my fifties that he began to pursue getting to know the real me. Therefore, I will do whatever it takes to avoid the feeling of abandonment. So whenever I am experiencing fear, I tell myself the truth: *God is always with me. I am never alone.*

Sometimes God will also provide the presence of another father figure in the body of Christ to supply our need for security. There were two specific times I experienced this. Once, while I was waiting to have thyroid surgery, several friends from church came and sat with us in the hospital waiting area. Anxiety gripped my heart — until the fatherly senior pastor arrived. His presence calmed me, and I knew everything would be okay. Another instance was when a crisis hit our family and I went to see the counseling pastor and his wife. As soon as I saw him, I lost it and wept. I could release my grief, knowing I could depend on him to help take care of us.

> How has God, your Father, displayed closeness to you?

Second, our Father God is **attentive.** He's awake, watchful, and aware of everything that goes on. "Indeed, he who watches over Israel will neither slumber nor sleep."[2] I'm comforted in knowing that nothing slips by His attention. What's more, God not only has His focus on us, but He's also committed to and interested in us. He keeps track of the number of hairs on our head![3] Our heavenly Daddy notices everything about us and everything that concerns us. He's attuned to our every need. As a result, I feel known and understood by God, my Father, which also makes me feel loved by Him.

> Describe ways in which you've seen your heavenly Daddy be attentive to you.

Finally, God is **responsive** to us in a variety of ways. He's emotionally available to us and can emotionally connect with us. He sees our needs, and He acknowledges and meets every one of them. ("Your Father knows what you need before you ask him."[4]) Another comforting promise is this: "And my God will meet *all* your needs according to the riches of his glory in Christ Jesus."[5] Numerous scriptures also point to God being our place of refuge: the Bible tells us that He is our place of security and our safe haven, that we can run to Him in times of trial, and that He offers comfort and protection for our soul.

> Reflect on how God has been responsive to you.

Here are some other biblical truths about attachment that we must believe if we are to be secure:

- God is there for us, and we belong to Him.[6]
- We can count on God and depend on Him to come through for us and be our advocate.[7]
- God really does care about us.[8]
- We have God's approval and acceptance.[9]
- God believes in us and our capabilities, and He created us for a purpose.[10]
- We are good enough and worthy of God's love and protection, based on all Christ has done on our behalf.[11]
- We already have God's affection and attention; therefore, we don't need to earn it.[12]
- God is crazy about us![13]

Which of these attachment statements are difficult for you to believe? Ask God to help you understand these truths in your heart.

God is the ultimate attachment figure, because He is present, attentive, and responsive. And a secure and intimate relationship with God contributes to closer relationships with others.

## The Why and How of Attachment to God

It is important that we, as believers, have a healthy attachment to God. First of all, without attachment — or without the security of knowing that God is present, responsive, and attentive — we'll take matters into our own hands. Instead of relying on God to meet our deepest needs for security and protection, for example, we'll turn to idols, which *Merriam Webster* defines as "objects of extreme devotion." I have gone to food, books, and friends to comfort me. Others might turn to idols of power, possessions, prestige, or pornography. Regardless, instead of bonding ourselves to God, we bond ourselves to these idolatrous dependencies. They medicate and temporarily numb us but are merely substitutes for the real thing — true intimacy with God, which we could experience if only we went to Him.

Only God can truly fill the emptiness within. As Drs. Tim Clinton and Gary Sibcy, in their book *Attachments,* write,

> Jesus wants to be the first link in the attachment chain. He wants us to turn first to Him, not to our parents or our spouses or anyone else. And when we do, our lives become properly ordered. (When we) cultivate a more secure attachment with God — it helps us break free from addictions, and the discipline helps us find God as our safe haven and learn to use Him as our secure base.

The goal, therefore, is to become securely attached to God our Father. When that happens and something emotionally rocks us, we will run to God, not idols, to find our comfort and security. But how do we do this?

I have experienced God's presence, attentiveness, and responsiveness when I sit quietly before Him to listen to His voice. It's during those times that I become acutely aware that I am known by Him, and as a result, He becomes known by me. Dr. Curt Thompson in *Anatomy of the Soul* writes,

> The degree to which you know God, is directly reflected in
> your experience of being known by Him. Healthy attachment,
> as we know, emerges from contingent communication, in
> which two individuals, through both their spoken dialogue and
> non-verbal cues, each affirm the other as they interact.

The interchange that happens when I hear God's voice causes me to become securely attached to Him. That's why I have devoted the final chapter of this book to the spiritual exercise of hearing the voice of God. Listening to God's voice has connected me to Him more than any other spiritual discipline.

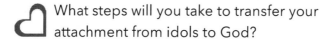 What steps will you take to transfer your attachment from idols to God?

## The Father Heart of God

*If you have seen me you have seen the Father.*

JOHN 14:9

God is the only perfect father we will ever know, and like the above verse states, when we look at Jesus, we see God the Father. Dr. David Stoop, in *Making Peace with Your Father*, writes that an effective father plays four roles: **nurturer**, **lawgiver**, **warrior/protector**, and **spiritual mentor**. Let's look at these roles in relation to God our Father according to Scripture, including the Gospel accounts of Jesus.

## The Four Father Roles in God

**Nurturers** exemplify the three characteristics of attachment behavior: they are present, they're in tune to the needs of others, and they respond. When I'm around a nurturer, I feel loved, valued, and secure. In the book of Mark, Jesus displays His nurturing aspect in the tenderness and value He showed to children.[14] Elsewhere in Scripture, our heavenly Father is described as merciful, tender, caring, loving, accepting, and sensitive; He listens and cares about how we feel; and He is called the "Father of compassion" and the "God of all comfort."[15] The Bible also identifies this nurturing side of God as part of His "mother heart," saying, "As a mother comforts her child, so will I comfort you; and you will be comforted over Jerusalem."[16]

I have found this nurturing side of God play out in real life. For instance, a friend of mine is encouraged any time she sees a red cardinal, as she takes it as a sign from God. Whenever I find a coin lying on the ground, I feel it is an indication that God is with me, cares for me, and knows me. It's as if God is whispering, "I'm here, right by you." Once, while on a mission trip, when at the Tanzanian airport, I found an American coin lying on the ground. In that moment, God's presence quelled my anxious thoughts as I prepared to fly to Mozambique. I have discovered other coins since then, sometimes at crucial moments and other times not, but the result is always the same: I feel loved by God and sense His presence.

The next role of God that shows His Father heart is that of **lawgiver.** The lawgiver aspect of Father God speaks to His authority, His integrity, and His ability to discipline. He gives us boundaries and discipline, not for our punishment but for our learning, with our benefit in mind.

When it comes to boundaries, it's not like God is saying, "I want to put a lid on your fun!" No, boundaries are for our protection and safety. God enforces them with our best interests in mind. Perhaps the best example of this is when the Pharisees asked Jesus what the greatest commandment was, and Jesus, our lawgiver, replied with "Love the Lord your God with all your heart and with all your soul and with all your mind. This is the first and greatest commandment. And the second is like it: 'Love your neighbor as yourself.'"[17]

Similarly, discipline is for our good: "But God disciplines us for our good, that we may share in his holiness. No discipline seems pleasant at the time, but painful. Later on, however, it produces a harvest of righteousness and peace for those who have been trained by it."[18] I personally never like the discipline experience while I'm in it. But after it's all said and done, I am eternally grateful for the fruit it has produced in me.

Our Father God is also a **warrior** and **protector**. This aspect of God is seen all throughout Scripture, in how He fights on behalf of His children, how He is always on our side, and how He wages war against our enemies. Exodus 15:3 declares, "The Lord is a warrior; the Lord is his name." And in the New Testament, Jesus is described as a heavenly warrior who will defeat the beast in the end times,[19] as one Who "lays down his life for the sheep,"[20] and as one Who came to "save his people from their sins."[21] This side of God gives us courage, as we know that we can have confidence in our Father God and His abilities.

My husband and I experienced God as the Warrior who came to our rescue when productivity in John's medical practice in Nebraska took a nosedive. Through a series of circumstances, God provided a position for him at a children's hospital in Kansas. Before we moved, God promised we would love what He had for both of us there. He was so right!

The protector side of God reminds me of the times when, as a little girl, I would watch *The Twilight Zone* or some other scary television show with my dad. When things became intense, you would find me on the floor in front of wherever Dad was sitting. I'd cover my face with my hands, barely peeking through the space between my fingers. As a little girl, I knew without a doubt that the safest place to be was near Dad. I had every confidence that he would protect me. And it is the same with God. When I trust that He is my protector, I can feel confident that there is no safer place to be than at His feet and in His will.

The last characteristic of God our Father is that of **spiritual mentor.** A mentor is "a trusted counselor or guide," according to *Merriam-Webster,* something similar to a coach. God's Word is full of spiritual truths that guide us in the best way to go.[22] The three years Jesus ministered, He showed mentorship when teaching spiritual truths, both to the masses, as seen in the Beatitudes,[23] and to small gatherings in the homes of His friends.[24] And after His death and resurrection, God the Holy Spirit, is known as Counselor. In my own life, God is my confidant, one with whom I entrust my deepest secrets. Like the psalmist David, I pour out my heart — the good, the bad, and the ugly — to Him.[25] In turn, my heavenly Father listens and gives me guidance. He understands me better than anyone else.

A final father role, which is not mentioned in Stoop's book, is that of **provider.** In most cases, children rarely fret over whether they will have enough food to eat or clothes to wear. They figure their parents will take care of those things. Likewise, when we recognize Father God as our provider, we can rest secure, knowing He will take care of all our needs. We see this role of God in Genesis 22:14, when He provides a lamb so that Abraham won't need to sacrifice his one and only son. And Jehovah-Jireh is the biblical name for God as provider.

> How have you seen Father God be your nurturer, lawgiver, warrior/protector, spiritual mentor, and provider?

Bob Mumford, in *The Agape Road: Journey to Intimacy with the Father,* expands on the provider role for both earthly dads and the Father God, saying fathers give their families **security**, **identity**, and **belonging** — security is the antidote for our fear, identity answers the question of who we are, and belonging deals with our need for acceptance.

In summary, we witness the Father heart of God when He fulfills the roles of nurturer, lawgiver, warrior/protector, spiritual mentor, and provider. And, in turn, we find our security, identity, and sense of belonging in being God's child.

> What is your image of Father God? Where does your image of Father God misalign with Who He portrays Himself to be through His Son, Jesus?

In Part 2, there is a chapter on knowing God that will cover more of His attributes, but for now, I encourage you to take time to list, on the left side of a piece of paper, your misconceptions of God the Father, based on the information you've read so far. Then on the right side, across from each misconception, write the corresponding truth and a scripture that supports it. Finally, declare out loud the truths you wrote as affirmations which will help them drop from your head into your heart.

# Forgiveness

*Bear with each other and forgive one
another if any of you has a grievance against
someone. Forgive as the Lord forgave you.*

COLOSSIANS 3:13

Even though my earthly dad wasn't without fault and unintentionally hurt me, he still held a special place in my heart. I continued to hope that, one day, he would become a Christian and we would have a close relationship.

Then in my mid-thirties, when I had a family of my own, my mom flew from Phoenix to visit us in Omaha. As usual, Dad did not come with her, since he feared flying. But when Mom returned to Phoenix, Dad picked her up at the airport, took her out to lunch, and informed her that after almost thirty-nine years of marriage, he wanted out. He had packed up his belongings while she'd been away.

My heart was broken when I heard that Dad had decided on divorce. I played Bob Fitts's song "Everything's Gonna Be Alright in Christ" on repeat, hoping that if I heard it enough, my upside-down world would become right-sided again.

Shortly thereafter, I met with two counselors at church. Both encouraged me to do the unthinkable: forgive my dad. Nothing in me wanted to do that! But then they shared applicable scriptures with me, and the Holy Spirit began to replay my past sins. I wept as I realized that after all of the sins God had forgiven me of, I must forgive my dad. So I chose to forgive him and to let him off *my* "hook," believing he was still accountable to God. I released him from having to pay me, Mom, and my sister back for how he'd hurt us. As far as I was concerned, Dad no longer had a debt to pay.

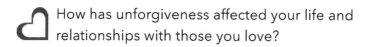 How has unforgiveness affected your life and relationships with those you love?

Once I forgave my dad, I learned that forgiveness is a gift we give ourselves. Because unforgiveness keeps us and our emotions bound by the offender — as if the offender is holding a rope wrapped around us, and whenever they jerk the rope, we react emotionally. In other words, unforgiveness keeps us emotionally enslaved to our offender. Bitterness, anger, and resentment toward an offender are all emotional signals that tell us we haven't offered forgiveness. When I haven't extended forgiveness, I am more likely to avoid eye contact with the person who has hurt me or to stay away from them altogether. At times, I even experience physical tiredness as a result of not processing my heart and extending forgiveness. But when I forgive the offender of their wrongdoing, the rope loosens and drops to the ground. The offender is still responsible to God for the sin, but I am no longer emotionally held captive by the offender or the hurt. When I see them again, the protective walls around my heart are down and I am free to be myself.

## The Fruits of Forgiveness

After my parents divorced, I became more intentional in pursuing a relationship with my dad. Soon after, the Lord gave me an "assignment" to make one of Dad's favorite baked goods for him on a regular basis. I did so, faithfully shipping him a package of cookies, coffee cake, or bread each month. Then, for one of his birthdays, I made him a "Daddy and Me" photo album. This included pictures of the two of us with A-through-Z words that described him. Another year, I put together an album with photos and letters that his friends and family wrote to him, recounting fond memories. I wanted my dad to feel loved and valued, and I hoped that God's kindness displayed through me would eventually lead Dad to repentance.[26]

A few years later, John and I had just returned from leading a team on a short-term mission trip to Mexico. My dad called as we walked in the door. Up to that point, Dad had rarely initiated a phone call with me. He had always gotten updates on my sister and me from Mom's calls. When I answered the phone, Dad asked, "How are you?" His showing concern for me was also foreign. After I got off the phone, I turned to John and said, "I'm thirty-seven years old, and I finally have a dad!"

Dad eventually visited us a few times in Omaha. He would drive the three days it took from Phoenix, and that in itself spoke volumes about how he loved and valued me. In contrast to what I had experienced as a little girl, I now knew Dad liked being with me. On one of Dad's visits, I told the Lord I really wanted my father's blessing. Even though Dad didn't have a personal relationship with Jesus, I knew God could answer my prayer.

That Sunday at church, during worship, our pastor held an altar call for those who wanted to lay down their burdens. I went forward and started to pray, but my heavenly Dad interrupted my outpouring and sweetly said, "Norma, you don't need your earthly dad's blessing. You have mine." I wept. I let go of all the expectations I had desired Dad to fulfill, and I released him.

At the end of that visit, Dad commented that it had been his best vacation. We hadn't done anything special, but I believed it was because he sensed I had no more expectations of him — and, as a result, he felt free to be himself.

Years later, at eighty years old, Dad was diagnosed with dementia and began to have regrets about his life. During that time, I flew to Arizona to help care for my mom after her heart-valve surgery. The day before my flight back home, my sister and I were to take Dad his favorite lunch. I sensed that God wanted me to share the salvation message with him again, but I was physically and emotionally exhausted. I had absolutely nothing left in me to give.

My sister and I picked up lunch at a restaurant, and as we started to leave the parking lot, we saw a ton of coins strewn across the lot. My sister, knowing about the significance of coins and God's presence in my life, jerked the car into a parking spot and rushed out to grab as much change she could fit into her pockets. I just sat in the car, stunned. After all was said and done, she had picked up over eleven dollars in coins, and there was still so much left! We couldn't stop giggling! God was highlighting His presence, showing us He cared.

At Dad's assisted-living residence, we sat down to have lunch in the backyard, and his dementia immediately kicked in, this time with paranoia. "You've got to contact the FBI!" he told us. "All of us here have been kidnapped!" But no sooner had those words left his mouth than his mind became sharp and tracked in normal conversation. For three more precious hours, Dad had a lucid mind.

So, I first brought up the subject of how to handle regrets. I told him that because I was a Christian, I could confess my sin and ask to receive God's forgiveness. Dad asked me what I had done to receive salvation. I briefly went through the steps. Then the next-door neighbor's mowing became too loud, so we went back inside to his corner bedroom. I had Billy Graham's tract *Steps to Peace with God*, so I started to read through it aloud with Dad. When I got to the part of praying the sinner's prayer, I asked Dad if he'd like to pray it with me. He said, "Yes!"

Phrase by phrase, Dad repeated the words after me. It was March 19. Exactly forty years earlier, I had accepted Christ as my Lord and Savior. I had prayed for my dad's conversion for forty years.

After he prayed, his countenance radiated. I took pictures of him smiling, and I will always remember the peace and freedom I saw on his face.

We may not always see such visible fruit from our forgiveness, but we must forgive anyway. Forgiveness is an act of obedience — we forgive because Jesus has forgiven us and because God asks us to. And when we do, we reap the benefits of peace within our hearts and at least some likelihood of reconciliation.

I am eternally grateful for the privilege of leading my dad to Christ. My forgiveness toward my dad paved the way not only for his salvation but also for my ability to have a closer relationship with him. I ended up having no regrets in my relationship with Dad, and I finally felt I possessed the position of Daddy's Girl.

Describe a time when God turned a painful memory around and redeemed it for your good and His glory.

. . . . . . . . . . . . . . . . . . . . . . . . . . . . . . .

## Reframing My Memory of Abandonment

I sit on the church pew at my wedding rehearsal, after hearing Mom's pronouncement that Dad might not walk me down the aisle. I see my heavenly Bridegroom, Jesus, sit down next to me. He places His right arm around my shoulder, takes my hand in His, and says, "Don't worry, my daughter, for I will be with you no matter what your dad decides to do. It will be you and me walking down the aisle, hand in hand, together." I feel strengthened by God's presence, knowing He is with me.

## What I Heard My Father Say

*You will never be alone, for I am always with you. No longer will you feel the effects of abandonment, for you are firmly attached to me. You will always be my child! There is nothing you could ever do or say to make you lose your position as my son or daughter. That's who you will forever be to me!*

**Take time to wait before the Lord.**
**Ask Him what He wants to say to you regarding this chapter.**

## ~ The Heart of the Matter ~

- Emotional wholeness is a means to an end — the end being intimacy with God.
- Our emotional overreactions to situations hint that there is an unhealed wound in our heart.
- Our inaccurate perceptions about what God is like can stem from painful relationships with our earthly parents.
- You can't give away what you don't possess.
- God is the ultimate attachment figure, because He is present, attentive, and responsive.
- A secure and intimate relationship with God contributes to closer relationships with others.
- God fulfills the four roles of fathers: He's a nurturer, lawgiver, warrior/protector, and spiritual mentor. He is also our provider and offers security, identity, and belonging.
- Forgiveness is a gift you give yourself.
- God takes the hurt in our lives and redeems it for our good and His glory.

## — 2 —
# ACCEPTED

*To the praise of the glory of his grace, by*
*which he made us accepted in the Beloved.*

EPHESIANS 1:6 (NKJV)

"I choose Peggy."

"Tom."

"Ginger!"

*Oh no. Please don't choose me last.*

"Mike, please."

"I want Jennifer!"

On and on it went, one name after another, until finally I was the only kid left. I gazed at the ground and waited for the words that always hurt more than anyone realized: "I guess we're stuck with Norma." Everyone giggled.

While I knew I wasn't athletic, that didn't stop me from feeling like a liability every time I was the last one chosen for a team in gym class. This was on top of the fact that, outside of gym class, my schoolmates often taunted me by saying, "You look like Jimmy Durante!" Durante, a singer and comedian in the fifties and sixties, had the nickname "the Schnozzola," in reference to his large nose. Large noses ran in my Syrian heritage — yet another opportunity for kids to make fun of me. Thus, seeds of rejection were planted within my heart at school, adding to those already sown at home. And when their roots sprouted, they grew long and deep, leading me to believe I was not wanted.

 How did rejection first enter your heart?

# Rejection

*He was despised and rejected by mankind, a*
*man of suffering, and familiar with pain.*

ISAIAH 53:3

Rejection is the "feeling of not being loved or wanted by another person," says H. Norman Wright in *Making Peace with Your Past*. Rejection can originate from various sources. On the home front, rejection can come from parents who favor one child over another. Parents overly busy with work and commitments can become emotionally detached or show little affection to their children, also leaving a mark of rejection. Cliques, whether at school, at church, or in the workplace, can make others feel they don't belong. And, as in my experience, kids who make fun of schoolmates can plant seeds of rejection.

 How have you experienced rejection in your life?

Rejection is a common struggle. The Bible alone is full of rejection stories: starting in Genesis, Cain's offering was rejected; the shepherd boy David was rejected for King Saul by the people; and Hagar was rejected by Sarai. Even our Savior, Jesus Christ, experienced rejection. Isaiah 53:2b-3 describes this well: "He had no beauty or majesty to attract us to him, nothing in his appearance that we should desire him. He was despised and rejected by mankind, a man of suffering, and familiar with pain. Like one from whom men hide their faces he was despised, and we esteemed him not." Nazareth, the city where Jesus spent his childhood, rejected Him.[27] His own biological brothers didn't believe Him.[28] One of Jesus's closest friends, Peter, rejected and denied knowing Him prior to His crucifixion.[29] And another disciple, Judas, betrayed Him.

# The Rejection Cycle

*Accept one another, then, just as Christ accepted
you, in order to bring praise to God.*

ROMANS 15:7

Derek Prince, in *God's Remedy for Rejection*, writes, "The primary result of rejection is the inability to receive or communicate love." Why? Rejected people — like all people — want acceptance and intimacy, but because they fear further rejection, they keep others at a distance. In essence, *they reject others,* and in doing so, they keep their desire for love and acceptance from being met. This is the rejection cycle.

John Paul Jackson, in *Breaking Free of Rejection*, describes the rejection cycle this way: "People who are overpowered by rejection expect to be over-looked and then create further rejection by being so negative and critical that no one enjoys being around them."

What Prince and Jackson are both saying is that rejected people reject people, thus inflicting more rejection upon themselves, and the cycle repeats itself. In other words, when we feel rejected and act out of that rejection using behaviors that offend others, it just invites more rejection — the very thing we dread and are trying to avoid.

I have seen this happen in my own life. Whenever I experience rejection, I want to erect walls around my heart to protect myself from being hurt again. It's like I build a castle, complete with a moat, to keep a "safe" distance from others.

In retrospect, I can also see how this played out in my dad's life and made an impact on me, creating a kind of generational rejection cycle. Because he struggled with rejection himself, he tried to find acceptance with his friends, which left him little time to spend with his daughters. As a result, while I knew Dad loved me, I didn't think he liked me because he didn't spend time with me (after all, people spend time with those they enjoy). I didn't feel special to my dad or like I had his attention — and in this way, rejection entered my heart.

# Responses to Rejection

*And so, we know and rely on the love God has for us.*

1 JOHN 4:16A

Although the Bible recounts stories of many people who were rejected, not all of them responded with wisdom. When Cain's offering was rejected and his brother's was accepted, Cain murdered his brother.[30] And when the people favored the shepherd boy David over King Saul in 1 Samuel 18, Saul tried to kill David.

On the other hand, when Abram's concubine Hagar was mistreated by Sarai, Abram's wife, she fled to the wilderness where she encountered God as *El Roi,* which translates to "the God who sees you."[31] And in the ultimate example, Jesus, after being beaten, was described in this way: "When they hurled their insults at him, he did not retaliate; when he suffered, he made no threats. Instead, he entrusted himself to him who judges justly."[32]

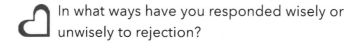 In what ways have you responded wisely or unwisely to rejection?

## Judgments and Vows

Rejection hurts. And while there are many possible responses to that hurt, the Bible encourages us to "commit ourselves to our faithful Creator and continue to do good" whenever we suffer.[33] Unfortunately, how we actually respond often plays out much differently, and we end up closing ourselves off from God and others.

One way that we do this is by making judgments and vows. A **judgment** is a generalized belief we form based on a specific event. For example, because my dad didn't intentionally spend time alone with me, I made the judgment, "He must not like me." (I'm having an "aha moment" as I write these words: this judgment is the reason I prioritize having time alone with each of my kids when they come to visit. I want them to know they're loved and valued by me.)

Making a judgment against the offender can, in turn, lead to our making a vow. A **vow** is a promise we make to ourselves, either knowingly or unknowingly, to live a certain way that we think will prevent future hurt. Here are some typical vows:

- "I am never going to let anyone get close to me."
- "I'm going to protect myself from rejection by keeping my distance from people."
- "I'm not going to share my heart, or I'll just get hurt again."

Thom Gardner in *Healing the Wounded Heart* writes this about vows: "A self-promise is an agreement with ourselves that binds us. The promises we make to ourselves usually show up in the way we live, and they become an operating system that governs our lives."

Unfortunately, vows do little to protect us; instead, they only perpetuate our rejection and loneliness, pushing us further into the cycle of rejection and away from true intimacy. To break the rejection cycle, then, we must keep judgments and vows at bay. The first step to doing this is to become aware of the pain we have as the result of rejection.

Becoming aware of pain isn't the most welcome task, but when I think back to my own experience, I wish I had been aware of my hurt from rejection sooner. If I had, I wouldn't have formed my own judgments and vows, thereby rejecting others and causing them pain. For instance, because I thought acceptance from others was based on performance, I tried to gain acceptance, both from myself and from people at church, by being overly involved in Christian ministry — and I'm sure my busyness resulted in my kids sometimes feeling rejected. When I became aware of the hurt I was holding as the result of feeling rejected, however, I realized how much it controlled my thoughts, words, and actions. And only then was I able to pursue my liberty.

Another step in breaking the strongholds of our vows and judgments is to renounce them. Part of *Merriam-Webster's* definition of *renounce* is to "give up, refuse to follow or obey." In this case, we can do that through repentance. When we repent, we confess our wrong in believing the lie (or judgment) and making the vow, and we seek God's forgiveness. In the first example of a vow

("I'm never going to let anyone get close to me"), after we confess it as sin and receive God's forgiveness, we can then declare the corresponding truth: "I will choose to let people get close to me, knowing God is my protector."

> Ask the Holy Spirit to reveal to you any vows or judgments you've made. Renounce them through repentance.

## When Judgments and Vows Become Characteristics

Although rejection is a common challenge, some of us struggle with it more than others. As a result, we have formed many judgments and vows, and we tend to display certain characteristics. I have observed these characteristics both in myself and others, and I learned more about them in John Paul Jackson's *Breaking Free of Rejection*.

People who struggle with rejection more than others often have the following attitudes and behaviors as a result of their vows and judgments:

- They are negative and pessimistic.
- They think others are always trying to hurt them.
- They are critical of themselves and judgmental of others.
- They are defensive when questioned or criticized.
- They are prideful, opinionated, and argumentative and will try to prove themselves right.
- They have a poor self-image and put themselves down.
- They seek security by getting attention — either positive or negative.
- They are oversensitive — easily hurt and protective of themselves.
- They withdraw and emotionally isolate themselves to prevent future rejection.
- They fear intimacy because they think it's too good to be true.
- They overvalue praise from others.

- They fear man and have difficulty being honest.
- They anticipate others will reject them.
- They avoid the risk of taking responsibility or trying things they don't excel in.
- They are dictatorial, bossy, or controlling.
- They feel compelled to convince themselves and others of their value (e.g., by name-dropping or bragging).
- They are self-absorbed and inwardly directed, not focused on others.
- They have a performance mindset, believing their acceptance is based on their performance.
- They have self-pity and a victim mentality, thinking they're always right.
- They seek affirmation and constantly demand attention.
- They go after approval, no matter the cost.
- They have one-way, codependent relationships.

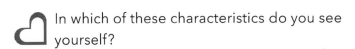 In which of these characteristics do you see yourself?

## My Own Responses to Rejection

Rejection prevents us from embracing and loving who we are and keeps us from fulfilling God's destiny for our lives. Some of the various outcomes of rejection in my own life, based on the lies I believed, were loneliness, fear of man, low self-worth, self-rejection, and tying my value to performance, approval, and acceptance. Feeling like I didn't fit in or belong, thinking very little of myself, and having the mentality of a victim were other reactions. But worst of all, my reactions to rejection prevented me from having close relationships with God and others. Fortunately, I also learned the truths I could use to fight the lies that had formed the basis of my negative reactions.

RESTORING YOUR HEART TO DEEPEN INTIMACY

## Needing Approval from Others

Further evidence of a struggle with rejection is **addiction to approval** and **the need to be liked by everyone.** My fear of rejection led me to become this way. I was a **people pleaser** and would strive for **peace at any price.**

Another way to describe these types of approval responses is to say I had the **fear of man,** which the Bible calls a "snare."[34] Bob Sorge, in *Dealing with the Rejection and Praise of Man,* says, "The one you fear is the one you will seek to please." When we fear man, we seek to please man — and this usually leads to dishonesty. In my own life, it prevented me from speaking the truth in love.[35] I found it hard to be honest whenever I wanted to say something that might hurt someone's feelings. And because I always wanted to be liked and accepted, I ran from confrontation and avoided conflict.

Yet another way I thought I could earn the approval of others was through **performance.** I thought that if I could just perform well enough, people would like me. I strived to be the best wife and mom, and I placed confidence in my flesh instead of in what Christ did for me on the cross.[36] I also always wanted to be "user-friendly" and **loathed asking people for help.** I believed the lie that if I required something from someone, that person wouldn't like or accept me.

What are your reactions to feeling rejected? Describe a time when your fear of man prevented you from obeying God.

A couple of experiences, in particular, revealed to me my need for others' approval. In the first instance, I felt devastated when I didn't receive the affirmation I had expected from a male ministry leader. My reaction — yearning for approval from a male authority — told me that, deep down, I was still in pursuit of my earthly dad's acceptance. In the second instance, I woke up one morning, suddenly feeling like I didn't belong. I felt misunderstood even by those closest to me, as if they really didn't know me. Years of painful rejection seemed to accumulate upon my heart that morning, and I couldn't stop the tears. I received ministry that night at our house church, but the next morning I still felt raw and couldn't control my emotions. As the pain of rejection resurfaced, however, the Holy Spirit whispered, *"If I were the only one who accepted you, would I be enough?"* Through tears, I said, "Yes."

### Declaring the Truth about Approval

The apostle Paul calls us to account regarding approval addiction: "Am I now trying to win the approval of human beings, or of God? Or am I trying to please men? If I were still trying to please people, I would not be a servant of Christ."[37] Similarly, in John 12:43, the apostle John describes the Jewish leaders with these words: "For they loved human praise more than praise from God."

When we know we have God's approval, we don't need to seek approval from man. After all, what God thinks of us is more important than what others think. Rejection can thwart our intimacy with God, however, making us feel as if God has rejected us — when in reality, He is our biggest fan.

Fortunately, we don't have to perform in a certain way or at a certain level to win our Father's approval. Consider this: The Father's approval and blessing of His Son, Jesus was not founded upon what Jesus did or how well He performed in ministry. When the prophet John the Baptist baptized Jesus before the start of His ministry, a voice from heaven said, "You are my Son, whom I love; with you I am well pleased."[38]

Likewise, our heavenly Father loves and accepts us even before we obey Him or do anything for Him. We also see proof of this in Romans 5:8: "But God demonstrates his own love for us in this: While we were still sinners, Christ died for us." The love of God compelled Him to die for us when we were at our worst, not when we got our act together and perfectly obeyed Him.

Both of these biblical accounts show us that our heavenly Father approves of us not because of who we are but because of who He is. Along these same lines of thinking, if your pain is from the rejection of an earthly parent, "begin to accept that your parents' not loving you is a statement about them and not about you," says H. Norman Wright in *Making Peace with Your Past*. "It bespeaks a defect in their ability to love rather than a defect in your lovability." In other words, when it comes to both our heavenly Father and our earthly parents, their acceptance of us has nothing to do with what we've done or who we are; it has only to do only with them.

Finally, we can remember that asking someone for help actually shows value to the other person. We all need to be needed, so requesting assistance and indicating that we need another person can encourage closer relationships. To equate asking for help with the fear of rejection is the enemy's deception, frustrating our desire for closeness.

> Are you addicted to the approval of man, or is God's approval your main motivation?

## Feeling Alone

Loneliness can take many forms. I have been afflicted with feeling like I **don't fit in**. I also identified with the odd duck in the *Ugly Duckling* fairy tale, thinking I **didn't belong**. David describes his **loneliness** by saying no one is concerned for him or cares about his life.[39] We can be in a room full of people and still feel lonely if there is no heart-to-heart connection.

### Declaring the Truth about Loneliness

Elisabeth Elliot, in *The Path of Loneliness*, says, "Our hearts are lonely till they rest in Him who made us for Himself." She encourages us to "see loneliness as a gift to be received, and to be offered back to God for His use."

Further, in Hebrews 13:5, God affirms, "Never will I leave you; Never will I forsake you." When we accept Jesus Christ as our Lord and Savior, His presence is always with us. Our loneliness is dulled or wiped away when we understand this.

> How have you experienced the effects of rejection in your life? In what ways have your relationships with God and man been influenced by rejection?

## Rejecting Ourselves

When we don't like our looks, personality, intelligence, weaknesses, or how we think or feel, we are **rejecting ourselves**. Having such **low self-worth, self-hate,** and dislike for myself were reasons I didn't set boundaries and allowed people to walk all over me. I believed I didn't deserve to be treated well, so I didn't take care of myself by putting boundaries in place.

In addition, for many years, my inner critic's words condemned me. Words are powerful. Proverbs 18:21a says, "The tongue has the power of life and death." And just as we are all hurt by others' careless words, we are also hurt by our own **self-criticism**. We believe what we tell ourselves, regardless of whether it is false or damaging.

On the other side of the self-rejection coin is a **victim mentality**, which can be the result of experiencing rejection over and over again. With this mentality, a "poor me" attitude and a belief that everyone is out to get us renders us hopeless, and we feel entitled, thinking everyone owes us. We fail to accept responsibility, and we pass the blame onto others, all while rationalizing our way out of our problems.

### Declaring the Truth about Self-Rejection

God has since convicted me of my sin of **self-rejection**. Self-rejection is a one-way street to destruction, and it plays right into the enemy's hand for his purpose to steal, kill, and destroy.[40] Now, when I make an error, I am kinder toward myself, thinking, *I made a mistake, but I'll do better next time.*

Brené Brown encourages us to talk to ourselves as we do with those we love. For example, I would never call a friend "stupid," yet I've said to myself aloud, "I am so stupid!" I'm grateful for my friends who hold me accountable and won't allow me to talk negatively about myself.

God also holds me responsible and won't let me put myself down. In fact, one day, while driving home after having lunch with a friend, I heard Him say, *"Stop selling yourself short, because when you do, you're selling Me short as well. When you put yourself down or highlight a weakness or negative habit in your life, it's as if you're saying that about Me. When you put yourself down, you're putting Me down, because I, the Creator, live within you."*

Further, Psalm 139:14 says we are "fearfully and wonderfully made." And in Matthew 19:19, God instructs us to "love your neighbor as yourself." This second verse suggests that the only way we can love and accept others is if we first love and accept ourselves (remember, we can't give away what we don't possess).

God accepts us just as we are. He knows each weakness we have and each sin we've committed (and will commit), and yet He still loves and accepts us. Why, then, shouldn't we also still love and accept ourselves?

Do you cheer yourself on in life, or do you put yourself down? Thank God for how He has created you.

# Rejection's Antidotes

*I have loved you with an everlasting love; I*
*have drawn you with loving-kindness.*

JEREMIAH 31:3

Rejection, like a poisonous vine, entangles all our relationships. In fact, it affects every aspect of life. It entwines itself in our jobs and families. It chokes off our intimacy with people and God. We pass on to others the rejection we have experienced, perpetuating the cycle of rejection indefinitely — that is, until healing comes to counteract the effects of the vine's poison. But to receive this healing, we require two antidotes.

## Antidote #1: Receive the Father's Unconditional Love, Acceptance, and Approval

I always told my children, "There is nothing you could ever do or say to make me stop loving you." My love for them is not dependent upon their obedience. I love them because they're my children. Similarly, there is nothing in our past, present, or future, nothing that we could ever do or say, to make our heavenly Father stop loving us. He loves us because we belong to Him and we are His children.

God's love for us is based on His nature. We are acceptable to God because of Jesus and what He did for us. Bob Sorge, in *Dealing with the Rejection and Praise of Man,* writes, "He accepts you because of who He is, not because of who you are." He loved us enough to send His one and only Son to die for our sins.[41] Jesus's death and resurrection are proof of our worth. God declares our value through His acceptance of us. We just need to receive it.

Because acceptance rooted in the cross depends not on our performance but on the sinless life of Jesus, it gives us stability.[42] Knowing that I am acceptable just as I am and that I don't have to earn God's acceptance frees me from my addiction to man's approval. I no longer have to perform to attain God's acceptance; I simply receive it and thank Him for it. Feeling accepted by God diminishes my need to be accepted by people, which frees me to be myself.

## Antidote #2: Love and Accept Yourself

What God says about us defines who we are, and His approval is what makes us feel secure. So when I struggle with self-rejection, I respond with these four steps:

- I rest in my significance and identity as Christ's child.

- I agree with God regarding how He sees me.

- I look to God for His approval and acceptance — that is, for everything I wish I'd received from my parents, spouse, children, boss, or friends. God alone becomes my source of acceptance.

- I don't believe lies but, instead, trust God's truth, found in the Bible.

We'll cover the topic of renewing our minds in a later chapter, but for now, here are some scriptures you can meditate on that counteract the lies you may believe as a result of rejection.

- You are loved by God.[43]

- You are a child of God.[44]

- You are accepted in the Beloved.[45]

- You are chosen in Christ and are among a chosen people belonging to God.[46]

- God has adopted you.[47]
- You are an heir of God and coheir with Christ.[48]
- You are complete in Christ.[49]
- You give God pleasure.[50]

The choice is yours: be a victim, locked behind the prison bars of rejection, or a victor, enjoying the freedom that comes from believing in God's unconditional love and acceptance.

In Ephesians 3:17b-19, the apostle Paul expresses my heart's desire for each of us as we navigate being free from the entanglements of rejection: "And I pray that you, being rooted and established in love, may have power, together with all the Lord's holy people, to grasp how wide and long and high and deep is the love of Christ, and to know this love that surpasses knowledge — that you may be filled to the measure of all the fullness of God."

Remember, people don't determine our worth; God does.

How can you apply both antidotes to rejection in your life?

## Rejection Redeemed

*And we know that in all things God works
for the good of those who love him, who have
been called according to his purpose.*

ROMANS 8:28

Rejection can be seen as a gift! An acronym for GIFT is God's Intentional Fine-Tuning. I have seen over and over again how God takes my rejection and redeems it not only for my good but for the good of others. God allowed my rejection and suffering with loneliness to woo me so that I would find my acceptance in Him alone. This can become true for you as well. And when it does, when you come to that place, you will no longer *need* man's acceptance.

I love the story of Joseph in the book of Genesis. He experienced so much adversity, rejection, and injustice — through his brothers' hands, his boss's wife, and others. But despite Joseph's rejection and unfair treatment and hard experiences, he later proclaimed to his brothers, "You intended to harm me, but God intended it for good to accomplish what is now being done, the saving of many lives."[51]

Likewise, God has used my rejection to conform me to His image by working His humility and compassion within me.[52] He has chiseled away my rough spots with the tool of rejection by breaking my heart and making it more contrite. This has led me to forgive those who have rejected me and to realize that, through their hands, God has shaped me more into His likeness. And for that I am grateful.

How has God redeemed your rejection and used it for your good? Have you reached a point where you can view rejection as a GIFT?

. . . . . . . . . . . . . . . . . . . . . . . . . . . . . . .

## Reframing My Memory of Rejection

Jesus is one of the team captains. As the choosing process begins, Jesus looks right at me. Our eyes meet, and He points at me. "I choose you, Norma. I want you to be on my team." Astonished, I run to Him and stand behind Him, jumping up and down and exclaiming, "I'm chosen!"

The Lord in this scene communicates that He wants me! He accepts me as I am, even though I'm not the best. I feel loved, accepted, and wanted. I know I belong on God's team.

Likewise, the Lord wants you to be on His team. He loves and accepts you just the way you are — without any improvements. Even if you're weak and imperfect, God chooses you. Deuteronomy 7:6 says, "For you are a people holy to the Lord your God. The Lord your God has chosen you out of all the peoples on the face of the earth to be his people, his treasured possession." And according to Ephesians 1:5–6, "Having predestined us to adoption as sons by Jesus Christ to Himself, according to the good pleasure of His will, to the praise of the glory of His grace, by which He has made us acceptable in the Beloved." He chooses you because you are His child. You are His.

## What I Heard My Father Say

*My child, I have not rejected you, so why do you reject yourself? Come to me. Let me show you how I see you. Look at yourself through my eyes of love. I have forgiven you and extend my grace to you. Please give yourself grace and receive my forgiveness. For the burden of self-hate does not come from me but from the enemy, Satan. Do not listen to him. He is full of lies and accusations. Listen to me and my truth and believe what I say about you.*

*I have chosen you, and you are mine! I did not die for those who are worthless. You are of great value to me. See your worth and acknowledge your value this day and receive my unconditional love, acceptance, and approval, which has never been and never will be based on your actions. The cross set you free. Accept and love yourself today, for this is my desire for you.*

**Take time to wait before the Lord.**
**Ask Him what He wants to say to you regarding this chapter.**

# ~ The Heart of the Matter ~

- Rejection is feeling unloved and unwanted by another person.

- Rejected people reject people.

- Judgments and vows are byproducts of rejection.

- The cycle of rejection keeps us lonely.

- Self-rejection is just as crippling as rejection from others.

- Rejection may lead to approval addiction and fear of man.

- Rejection redeemed conforms us to the image of God.

- The remedies for rejection are receiving God's unconditional love, acceptance, and approval and loving and accepting ourselves.

- Rejection prevents us from embracing and loving who we are and keeps us from fulfilling God's destiny for our lives.

- Grasping God's acceptance of us diminishes our need to be accepted by people, which frees us to be ourselves.

- What God says about us defines who we are.

- God's approval makes us feel secure.

- What God thinks of us is more important than what others think.

— 3 —

# UNASHAMED

*Do not be afraid; you will not be put to shame. Do*
*not fear disgrace; you will not be humiliated. You*
*will forget the shame of your youth and remember*
*no more the reproach of your widowhood.*

ISAIAH 54:4

"Norma, you earned an *F* in reading this quarter."

Tears welled, but I wouldn't let them fall. *I must be a failure. After all, that's what* F *stands for.* I wanted to run away, but the compliant child within me kept my body glued to the chair until the fifth-grade parent-teacher conference finished. I had consistently forgotten to turn in my reading homework, and a failing grade had been the result. I held my breath and waited to hear the familiar words: "Shame on you!"

Describe your earliest recollection of shame.

John Paul Jackson describes shame in *Unmasking the Jeze-bel Spirit* as "the sense of feeling fundamentally bad, inadequate, defective, unworthy, or not measuring up to standards." Dictionary definitions of shame include the words "dishonor" and "disgrace." And in *The Search for Significance*, Robert McGee defines shame as "a deep sense of inferiority." In a nutshell, shame is whatever attacks our character and assaults our core being.

Have you ever heard your inner critic say, "I'm so stupid!" or "I'll never be good enough." Or what about "I'm not good at anything. I must be an awful person." Whenever we entertain wrong and negative perceptions of ourselves, shame is usually behind it all, permeating our every thought.

# The Set-Up

*Forget the former things; do not dwell on the
past. See, I am doing a new thing! Now it springs
up; do you not perceive it? I am making a way
in the desert and streams in the wasteland.*

ISAIAH 43:18–19

I lived under the veil of shame most of my life, and more than any other obstacle, it kept me from being close to the Lord. It has also prevented my intimacy with others and hindered me from being the person God created me to be.

Growing up with a critical and moody dad, who allowed his emotions to dictate his actions and whose alcoholism made his behavior even more unpredictable, caused my sister and I to go straight to Mom after school each day to ask what kind of mood Dad was in: Should we be cautious that day, walking on the proverbial eggshells, or were we free to be our normal selves? Living in this home environment caused me to become fearful and insecure.

That, combined with being slightly chubby and never excelling in school, sports, or music, made me feel generally inferior and ashamed of who I was. My shyness and stuttering added to my embarrassment and confirmed what I already "knew": I wasn't special. Even though I couldn't articulate it at the time, I believed the following lies:

- I have to be perfect, or at least look like it, so people will like me.
- I need to stuff my negative emotions so that I appear to be okay.
- I have to do more and be more in order to be acceptable.
- I must not be special, or my dad would spend time with me.
- I must earn God's love through my performance.
- I must have everyone's love and approval.

In what ways is your past similar to mine? Identify the lies you've believed that have held you captive under shame.

## Shame's Entry Points

*Then the eyes of both of them were opened, and they realized they were naked; so they sewed fig leaves together and made coverings for themselves.*

GENESIS 3:7

Shame can enter into our hearts and minds through various avenues. Here are just a few of them:

- As a natural response when we sin
- As the result of sinful choices that others make against us
- As a reaction when parents are not physically or emotionally available to their children
- As the byproduct of physical, sexual, verbal, or emotional abuse
- As a result of real or perceived failure, whether at school, in ministry, in relationships, or at work
- As a response to unfulfilled dreams, desires, and expectations, and even loss
- As a reaction to forms of defectiveness caused by physical appearance, illness, or handicap

Through what avenues has shame entered your heart? What are some triggers or circumstances in life that make you feel defective as a person?

# Shades of Shame

*Then the man and his wife heard the sound of
the LORD God as he was walking in the garden
in the cool of the day, and they hid from the
LORD God among the trees of the garden.*

GENESIS 3:8

Adam and Eve's first reaction to feeling shame was to hide from God.[53] The same is true of us today: sin leads to shame. Shame causes us to fear rejection. And fear of rejection causes us to hide our true selves. For this reason, a good acronym for SHAME is Sinners Hiding All Mistakes Every day.

People's responses to shame come in various shades, but all are ways to hide their true selves. Typical emotional responses to shame are fear, anxiety, depression, and low self-esteem. Some people living in shame feel flawed, thinking something is wrong with them; these people often compete and compare themselves with others, hoping to reach the top rung of the ladder so they can feel better about themselves. Other people who feel ashamed become overly defensive when criticized or develop a victim mentality, blaming others for their mistakes instead of taking responsibility; these people can be self-focused and display selfish love, they typically don't take risks, and they procrastinate because of their fear of failure.

Hiding is exactly what I did too. One way I did this was through **performance**, as shame led me to get my sense of worth from doing, not from being. At home, I felt like the forgotten child and desperately wanted to be noticed, so I wore a "Miss Goody Two Shoes" label, obeying my parents just to receive their attention. I also performed through academic and professional achievement. In high school, I participated in numerous extracurricular activities and held various positions in clubs, and in college, I attained a master's degree instead of being content with a bachelor's. Then as a young mom, I became overly committed in ministry to the point of experiencing emotional burnout. I did all these things unconsciously to be accepted by my family, my friends, and myself. My very identity, who I thought I was, had come to depend upon my performance.

Another way I hid in shame was by **pretending** to be who others expected me to be. I was so ashamed of who I was that I feared if people knew the real me, they would reject me. And after time, I became so skilled at being who others wanted me to be that I forgot who I really was. I also grew up with the misbelief that I needed to be user-friendly, which meant I would do whatever anyone asked me to. I said yes too often, since I thought saying no would cause disappointment and rejection, and I rarely offered my opinion, instead readily agreeing with whatever others believed. People-pleasing thus became my *modus operandi*.

Since I didn't think I was good enough, I also attempted to cover my true self with **perfectionism**. I tried to appear perfect by always doing the right thing, hoping to prevent my flaws from being exposed. So even though I proclaimed to be a born-again believer, I became a modern-day Pharisee, trying to earn God's approval and acceptance through legalism. I thought that if I went to church regularly, spent time in God's Word daily, prayed often, and ministered to many, I would receive not only God's stamp of approval but man's. Being religious fed my pride, which hid the real issue: I felt that something was wrong with me.

I also hid from shame by wearing the cloak of a **rescuer**. I needed to be needed and to feel important. So I became overly responsible and codependent on others. Over-functioning and doing for others what they could do for themselves served to numb my pain from the past and from shame.

How do you hide or cover up your true self in order to be more acceptable to others, God, or yourself?

**Addiction and idolatry** were other ways I hid in shame. Instead of running into the arms of Jesus when I felt ashamed, I turned to food for comfort. And books became my friends to keep me from feeling lonely. An idol is whatever controls our attention, affection, time, or money more than God does. Drs. Clinton and Sibcy, in their book *Attachments*, say, "Even positive addictions and rituals like studies, sports and religious activities, can create a false sense of closeness in which habits and things replace our need for relationship."

However, Scripture tells us, "Those who cling to worthless idols turn away from God's love for them."[54]

What idols or addictions do you run to for comfort?

## Six Steps to a Shameless Life

*I sought the LORD, and he answered me; he delivered me from all my fears. Those who look to him are radiant; their faces are never covered with shame.*

PSALM 34:4–5

Several years ago, as I prepared to leave a counseling-leadership retreat, an older woman hugged me good-bye and said the two words that set the wheels in motion for my deliverance from shame: "You're special." For days, I replayed those words over and over in my mind, and soon I began to believe them.

A few days later, I attended a seminar on emotional burnout at a church in California. A worship leader joined us on the last day and sang quietly during ministry. While I was waiting to say good-bye to the women I had met, the worship leader approached me and said, "The Lord is asking me to do something I've never done before."

I looked at him and said, "Please do it." He played his guitar and sang *Jesus Loves You* to me. I wept. After he finished, he prophesied in a way that began to break pieces of shame off of my heart and to restore my honor. He said he had a vision of me standing under a shower that was cleansing me of sin and shame. The water from the shower ran down a dirt road and pooled at the foot of the cross. Next, he saw Jesus sitting at the head table at a banquet. I came in and sat at one of the tables in the back of the room. Jesus got up, came over to me, and had me sit next to Him at the head table.

This worship leader's prophecies marked the beginning of my process of healing from shame, revealing how, in God's eyes, I wasn't defective or worthless but one who had value. After that day, I slowly but surely began to believe this truth, and I continued to heal by learning and applying the following six steps.

## Step 1: Confess and repent your sins. Receive and offer forgiveness.

When shame is caused by our own sin, we must repent in order to heal. And when shame is brought on by someone's sin against us, we must forgive in order to heal.

### Repentance

A close friend once told me, "The only way to feel better is to feel bad first." When we have the bad feeling of shame as a result of sin, we can repent of the sin. Repentance is turning away from sin and turning toward God, seeking His forgiveness. Luke 13:3 says, "But unless you repent, you too will all perish." And when we "confess our sins, He is faithful and just and will forgive us our sins and purify us of all unrighteousness."[55] There is no sin too great that God cannot forgive and purify us from. And when He does, we will always feel better.

I used to cringe at the thought of repentance. I believed my need to repent only highlighted my defects and feelings of shame. But now I see it more from God's perspective. God knows that I feel guilty after I sin and that what's best for me is to be set free from my guilt, to accept His forgiveness in my heart, and to see my relationship with Him restored — and He enables all of this to happen by offering the opportunity of repentance. He has my best interest in mind, knowing that if I don't repent, my internal guilt will destroy me. As such, repentance is a gift from God. The Bible says He even leads us to repentance through kindness.[56]

In turn, when we accept this gift, genuinely repenting of our sin, we also receive peace and refreshment in our hearts. Just as peace is restored to my heart after I've cleaned my cluttered house, so too is peace reestablished after I've repented and decluttered my heart from sin. And Acts 3:19 says, "Repent, then, and turn to God, so that your sins may be wiped out, that times of refreshing may come from the Lord." I interpret *refreshing* as the freedom I experience when my sin is cleansed and my relationship with God is restored.

Periodically, I'll ask God to show me what's in my heart. I want the Holy Spirit to shine His light upon any unconfessed sin, and when He does, I immediately repent. The Lord taught me years ago that just as the easiest time to scrape dishes is immediately after they've been dirtied, the easiest time to repent is right after I've been convicted of my sin. If I wait and let the dirty dishes sit in the sink, the food will harden, making them more difficult to wash later. Likewise, if I wait to repent, pride will surely come in and harden my heart, convincing me that I don't need to be penitent.

When I repent, I'm agreeing with the psalmist when he wrote, "Create in me a clean heart, O God."[57] However, repentance is not just being sorry for the sin itself or even for its consequences; it is also grieving over how your sin has affected your relationship with God. As David prayed, "Against you, you only, have I sinned."[58] Genuine repentance is godly sorrow over your sin that also leads to a change in behavior.

Finally, while repenting of sin can free you from shame, you can also confess and repent of shame itself, praying, for example: "I confess the ways I've allowed my shame to make me hide from others. Please forgive me, Lord, for being overly responsible for others and for idolizing my ability to rescue them."

> What sin do you need to confess so that you can receive God's forgiveness and restore your relationship with Him?

*Forgiveness*

To make steps toward releasing ourselves from shame, we must also forgive those who have sinned against us. Jesus speaks to the importance of forgiveness when He says, "For if you forgive other people when they sin against you, your heavenly Father will also forgive you. But if you do not forgive others their sins, your Father will not forgive your sins."[59] That scripture gives me the motivation to forgive those who have hurt me, because I don't want anything to prevent my heavenly Father from forgiving me! As C. S. Lewis put it, "To be a Christian means to forgive the inexcusable, because God has forgiven the inexcusable in you."

When we forgive someone, we are essentially saying that we will not take revenge for the offense but will instead entrust our Father with our situation, with ourselves, and with our offender's justice. We are acting in the same way Jesus did: "When they hurled their insults at him, he did not retaliate; when he suffered, he made no threats. Instead, he entrusted himself to him who judges justly."[60] Forgiveness is a choice, not a feeling, and requires supernatural assistance from God. Sometimes it is also a process — not something that happens overnight. And finally, forgiveness is unconditional and requires nothing from the offender. When we truly forgive someone, we may not forget the offense like God does, but we will no longer hold it against them.

Take a few minutes to read the parable of the unmerciful servant in Matthew 18:21–35. Verses 21 and 22 show that there is no limit to the number of times we may need to forgive someone, while verse 27 gives us three components of offering forgiveness:

1. **Have compassion.** The master took pity on his servant. Having compassion on our offender, however, is not always easy. When I struggle to forgive someone and to have compassion on them, I remember those sins of which God has graciously forgiven me. Then I allow my gratefulness to humble me and encourage me to give to my offenders what I have freely received. We're instructed to "forgive as the Lord forgave you."[61] Freely we have received God's forgiveness; therefore, we need to freely give forgiveness away.

2. **Cancel the debt.** The master canceled the servant's debt so that the servant no longer owed the master anything. Likewise, when we forgive those who hurt us, we must let them off our hook, even though they are not off God's and will still be accountable to Him.

3. **Release the offender.** The master let the servant go. When we follow suit, we are essentially declaring that the offensive situation is a done deal and no longer controls our heart strings. It's this component of forgiveness that has led to the saying "Forgiveness is a gift you give yourself" — for when we forgive others, we set ourselves free. Conversely, not forgiving is like drinking poison and expecting the other person to die. The one who forgives always wins.

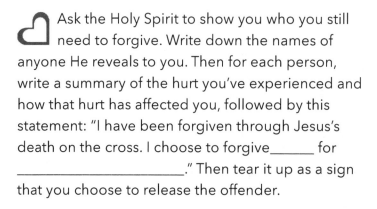

Ask the Holy Spirit to show you who you still need to forgive. Write down the names of anyone He reveals to you. Then for each person, write a summary of the hurt you've experienced and how that hurt has affected you, followed by this statement: "I have been forgiven through Jesus's death on the cross. I choose to forgive_____ for _____." Then tear it up as a sign that you choose to release the offender.

A few final words about forgiveness: forgiving someone does not mean you automatically restore trust with them. Trust needs to be rebuilt, which takes time. However, the adage "time heals all wounds" is false; rather, forgiveness heals all wounds. Sometimes it just takes time for our hearts to catch up to the choice we've made to forgive.

Finally, the Bible instructs us to bless and pray for those who have hurt us: "Bless those who curse you, pray for those who mistreat you."[62] As you pray for your offender's blessing, your heart will become more aligned with God's heart, and you will begin to see the offender through God's eyes of compassion.

By the way, I learned the value of forgiveness from a little booklet called *Processing the Issues of Your Heart*. This booklet has been invaluable over the years to help me move through the hurt of offense and loss to forgiveness which leads to freedom. The Fresh Start website is full of wonderful resources. You can find their link in my bibliography.

## Step 2: Realize righteousness is based on God's grace and on what Christ has done — not on anything you could ever do.

Shame is like a prison door that only God's grace can unlock. Fortunately, God gives His grace freely. Ephesians 2:8–9 says, "For it is by grace you have been saved by faith — and this is not of yourselves, it is the gift of God — not by works, so that no one can boast."

On the cross — the greatest symbol of God's grace — Jesus took our shame so that we could receive His grace. Pastor Bill Johnson of Bethel Church in Redding, California, explains it this way: "Jesus took what I deserved so I could get what He deserved." Therefore, when we accept His grace, it is as if our shame has been nailed to the cross with Him.

And how do we accept grace? It is by faith alone that we receive and open that gift. No level of perfection or performance on our part could ever grant us eternal life, peace, or contentment; we can't do anything to save ourselves. Romans 5:8 says God demonstrated His unconditional love for us not while we were performing at our very best but while we were at our worst. The cross is proof that God the Father loves us *just as we are*.

On the same token, if we don't receive God's grace, we are essentially sending the message that what Christ did on the cross was not good enough. When I lived a life of performance, it was like telling God that His suffering on the cross *plus* whatever I did would get me into heaven. Shame caused me to focus on myself — while the cross turned my focus onto Christ.

## Step 3: Replace the lies you believe about yourself with truth.

Remember that shame is usually the culprit behind any wrong and negative beliefs we have about ourselves. It permeates our every thought, assaulting the very core of who we are and convincing us we are fundamentally flawed. What's worse, however, is that we become what we think and believe about ourselves, because our actions tend to align with our thoughts. This makes it impossible to live beyond what we think and believe.

For instance, what if I held the belief that I had nothing to say that others wanted to hear? Most likely, I would not be a writer. Similarly, if I held the general belief that I was a victim, I would probably succumb to self-pity in my daily life. As Marianne Williamson says, "You must master a new way to think before you can master a new way to be." That's why we must replace the lies we believe with God's truth. In my own life, I have learned to replace the lie "I'm not good at anything" with the truth that "I'm good at many things. We all have strengths and weaknesses."

What lies are you believing?

## Step 4: Base your identity on who God is and who you are as His son or daughter.

Unashamed people don't have identity issues, because their identity and feelings of significance lie in being God's child. Thus they don't need anything to make them feel better about themselves. They don't need leadership positions in ministry or business to feel important. They don't need to hide behind masks when they present themselves to others. They know who they are and they're free to be themselves.

We'll dive deeper into the subject of identity in the second half of the book. But until then, we can remember that to fight shame, we must find our value not in our performance or in others' conditional love but in God's unconditional love and acceptance and in His finished work on the cross.

 What or who gives you value?

## Step 5: Understand your hurts and grieve your losses.

Shame can be a response to unfulfilled dreams, desires, and expectations, and even to loss. As such, shame can feel a lot like pain. Personally, I prefer to avoid pain at all costs. I would rather deny its existence, sweep it under the rug, and pretend it's not there. The problem with that is, eventually, it builds up, and I begin to trip over the lumps in the carpet. In the same way, undealt-with pain will accumulate, and when we least expect it, it will trip us up, catching us unaware.

This happened to me shortly after returning from a short-term mission trip to Kabul, Afghanistan. I was out on the back deck of our house when I heard a shot fired and saw a squirrel die. I ran up to my bedroom, sobbing. The shot had triggered my memory of hearing bombs and gunfire when the Taliban had tried to capture the city of Kabul, which led to my other memories of that trip: among them, malnourished children receiving food in the refugee line, and children in the hospital who had been maimed by picking up what they thought were toys but were explosives instead. I had not yet grieved my pain from seeing all of this; I had merely swept it under the rug. After I arrived home, my stuffed pain refused to stay hidden. Triggers are like indicators on the car's dashboard, signaling that something needs to be repaired. In this case, I needed to acknowledge my pain, grieve, and invite Jesus into my healing process.

Emotions, including pain and shame, are a gift from God. They help us understand not only ourselves but those around us. Dr. Curt Thompson, in *Anatomy of the Soul*, says that emotion "is the means by which we experience and connect with God, others, and ourselves in the most basic way possible." He goes on to write, "It is through the brain's medium of emotion that God most frequently addresses us. If we ignore, deny, or debate these feelings, we are ignoring God's messengers."

One of the best things we can do for ourselves is to give ourselves permission to feel, express, and deal with our emotions. It's necessary to weep over a loved one who is ill or has passed, to mourn rejection or betrayal by those closest to you, to lament over a job loss, or to experience disappointment when an expectation is not met. And when we have a negative emotion, such as hurt, it behooves us to acknowledge and deal with the feelings promptly. If we stuff them or put off dealing with them, we only delay the inevitable. Eventually, the hurt will come out.

Just as detrimental as not grieving our hurt is becoming stuck in or too comfortable with grief, unwilling to move on. It's not healthy when grieving becomes a destination — the final place we unpack our bags and make ourselves at home. Rather, grieving is meant to be a place we pass through when we're trying to get somewhere else. It's a helpful process by which we can transition from "what was" to "what will be." Grief is most beneficial when we keep moving through it.

*The Benefits of Processing Pain*

Listening to our hearts and giving ourselves permission to feel hurt can benefit us in several ways.

1. **Restoration can begin only when we acknowledge our hurt.** Pain tells us that something is wrong so that we can tend to it in an effort to heal and experience the freedom God intended for us. When we acknowledge pain, we take steps toward healing and freedom. But when we deny our grief and stuff it deep within our hearts, we keep ourselves from getting to the other side of hope.

2. **Grieving helps us move forward and not remain stuck in the past.** When we hold onto our pain, we fix our focus on the past, thus missing the present and whatever lies ahead. But when we grieve our pain and loss, release it, and then let it go, our hands open up so that we can fully embrace the gift God has for us next.

   I experienced this truth firsthand when I learned that would have to say good-bye to my comfortable and familiar life in Omaha, Nebraska, to move to Wichita, Kansas. God must have bottled up the tears I poured out to Him as He listened to my prayers. But through my grieving, I was able to cross the road into gratefulness, and it prepared my heart to receive all that God had waiting for me in Wichita.

3. **Grieving can bring us closer to God.** God promises that He is close to the brokenhearted.[63] Thus grieving can be a gift from God, deepening our relationship with Him through the comfort He provides.

 What losses do you need to grieve?

*Ways to Process Pain*

We each process loss differently. But the first crucial step for all of us is to embrace our pain by being aware of it and verbalizing it. Speaking out how we feel is like holding a mirror up in front of us; it shows a reflection of our hurt and helps us to "see" how our heart feels. This can be as simple as saying, "I feel sad" (or "lonely," "upset," or "angry.")

We can also verbalize our pain by pouring out our hearts to God in prayer. God already knows our hearts, but He wants us to pray as a way get in touch with them. He also wants us to share our hearts with Him as a way to commune and draw near to Him. As King David wrote, "Trust in him at all times, you people; pour out your hearts to him, for God is our refuge."[64] David also set a good example of this when he wrote, "I cry aloud to the Lord; I lift up my voice to the Lord for mercy. I pour out my complaint before him; before him I tell my trouble."[65]

As we process the hurt in our hearts with God, we can also ask him to be our heart's comforter and healer. (After all, one of the names the Bible gives to God is *Jehovah Rapha*, "the Lord is my healer.") This can be as simple as saying, "Father, I give you my pain. Comfort me as I grieve and let go of my hurt."

As I process my own hurt with God, I also write about the pain I'm feeling in a journal. The year we lived in Chicago for John's final year of medical training, I went through six journals. It was our first move away from Arizona, and I struggled with loneliness, living out of my comfort zone in a big city, and being like a "single parent" of a four- and two-year-old while John worked long hours. God was my counselor and confidant, faithfully helping me through that hard year as I daily poured my heart out to Him in my journal.

Other ways we can share our hearts is by sitting with a friend or confidant over coffee, talking with our spouse, or walking on a treadmill next to a friend while processing the hurt within. This can be particularly helpful for those who are verbal processors, as I am — I often gain understanding of my pain as I describe my feelings to someone who listens and validates.

## Step 6: Put your hope in God, the One who wants you to be restored and transformed.

God promises in Psalm 25:3, "No one who hopes in you [God] will ever be put to shame." We can put our hope in God because we can be certain that He will ultimately use our shame — along with any associated sin, addiction, insecurity, or other hurt — for our good and His glory. For once we are delivered from the prison of shame, we become free to be who God created us to be; our lives become marked by intimacy with God and others; fear, pride, and selfish ambition have less power over us; our identity no longer resides in our position, performance, or possessions; and we become empowered by God — and for all of this, He will receive greater glory.

But the choice is ours: we can choose to live under shame, playing the victim and trying to hide behind masks, or we can choose to put our hope in God, receiving His grace through faith and remembering that we will never be "good enough" based on what we do but based solely on what Christ has done for us on the cross.

What are you waiting for? Receive God's promise: "Instead of your shame you will receive a double portion, and instead of disgrace you will rejoice in your inheritance. And so you will inherit a double portion in your land, and everlasting joy will be yours."[66] Pray, "I place my hope in You alone, God. Restore me and transform me to look more like Your Son, Jesus." Then thank God for all He's done. Begin to walk in freedom with your head held high rather than under the cloak of shame.

. . . . . . . . . . . . . . . . . . . . . . . . . . . .

## Reframing My Memory of Shame

I am at my fifth-grade parent-teacher conference. Jesus stands behind me, His left hand on my shoulder. As the teacher drops her gavel and declares my *F* in reading, I turn my head and glance up at Jesus, fearful that His face will show anger with me. Instead, I see eyes full of compassion. Jesus opens His mouth and speaks: *"This is not who you are. You are not a failure. I know your capabilities, for I have formed you in your mother's womb, and I know how intelligent I made you. Again, my daughter, this is not who you are. Work on your reading assignments, and you'll turn that grade around in no time. It will take work, and I will remind you to get it done. You are my daughter, and no child of mine needs to be ashamed. Now go and play on the playground. Have some fun. But first, remove your cloak of shame and leave it on your folding chair. I will dispose of it."*

## What I Heard My Father Say

*Oh, my child, how I have loved you with an everlasting love. The enemy has come to rob, steal, and destroy your innocence, leaving upon you a cloak of shame, but I say to you this day, "Shame be off of you!" When you are convicted of sin, simply confess and repent. Wholeheartedly embrace My forgiveness, which I bought for you on the cross.*

*Lay down your cloak of performance. Lay down the various ways you comfort yourself instead of running into my arms. Lay down your idols. Lay down anything you do to try to earn my acceptance and approval. For my sons and daughters already have that. Unwrap my unconditional gift of grace and receive honor in the place of shame.*

*Now go. You are free to be yourself.*

**Take time to wait before the Lord.**
**Ask Him what He wants to say to you regarding this chapter.**

## ~ The Heart of the Matter ~

- Shame is a deep sense of inferiority. It attacks our character and assaults our core being.
- Shame permeates our thoughts when we entertain wrong perceptions of ourselves.
- Shame causes us to hide our true selves, which prevents us from being who God created us to be.
- We cover up our shame through performance, pretending, perfectionism, rescuing, and idolatry.
- Even good things can become like little gods to us.
- Repentance is a gift from God, and the easiest time to repent is immediately after we're convicted.
- Forgiveness is a gift we give ourselves, because it releases our heart from the control of the offense and the offender.
- There is no sin too great that God cannot forgive.
- The gift of God's grace releases us from shame.
- The cross is proof that God loves us just as we are.
- Loss needs to be grieved.
- We become what we think and believe. Our actions line up with our thoughts, so it is impossible to live beyond what we think.
- Unashamed people don't need anything to make them feel less ashamed.

# — 4 —
# BRAVEHEARTED

*Have I not commanded you? Be strong
and courageous. Do not be terrified; do
not be discouraged, for the Lord your God
will be with you wherever you go.*

JOSHUA 1:9

When I was growing up, my mom, sister, and I would visit my aunt on Saturday mornings. On one of these visits, I must have been dillydallying in the car, because before I knew it, I was the only one left. I got out of the car and walked into the house. But the furniture was all different.

"Oh, no," I whispered. "This isn't Aunt Mary's house. I have to get out of here!"

Panic rose in my heart as thoughts rushed through my five-year old mind. *What if the people who live here find me? I don't want to get in trouble!* I ran out to my mom's car and hid in the back seat. Crouching on the floor and covering my head with my arms, I hoped no one could see me. My heart raced, terrified that I would be discovered and punished, yet also frightened to be alone.

Fear entered my little girl's heart that day, and now whenever I find myself trapped and frightened, I still want to run away and hide. I'm tempted to escape the scary situation and find safety in a protective place.

 Describe your earliest recollection of fear.

# Fear Fleshed Out

*Fear of man will prove to be a snare.*

PROVERBS 29:25A

*Webster's 1828 American Dictionary of the English Language* defines fear as "A painful emotion or passion excited by an expectation of evil, or the apprehension of impending danger. Fear is accompanied with a desire to avoid or ward off the expected evil."

My dad used to say, "Fear is the most powerful emotion," and I tend to agree. Because whether perceived or real, fear has the ability to direct our very lives. It can force us into the back seat, grab hold of our steering wheel, and drives us wherever it wants to go. It can also immobilize us, stopping us dead in our tracks.

At nine years old, I went away to Girl Scout camp. The second time I sat on a horse, another horse got spooked, and I found myself in the middle of a stampede. I dropped the reigns, fell off the horse, and hit my head on a rock. After a night alone in the hospital, the Girl Scout counselors tried to get me back on a horse. I was terrified, so they had me ride a donkey. At subsequent camps, I came equipped with a letter from my physician giving me permission not to ride the horses. Thirty years later I got back on a horse. Without a doubt, fear cripples.

Fear goes by a number of different names — *anxiety, worry,* and *concern,* just to name a few. Fear also shows up in a variety of ways. For example, even though I'm rather outgoing now, I was shy growing up. I was too **timid** to talk to the telephone operator over the phone or to meet new people. I also **stuttered** to get my words out when asking questions.

When I was in sixth grade, my mom even promised me a pair of go-go boots if I stopped my **nervous habit** of biting my nails for two weeks. Being motivated to get in on the craze of the day, I exercised self-control and ceased my biting. Two weeks later, I strutted to school wearing my shiny, new white boots. My self-control didn't last long though, because the next time I became **anxious,** I started chewing my nails again.

A few other times when I was young, my parents would go out of town, leaving my older sister and me in the care of a sitter. I would **feel abandoned** during those times, my stomach twisted in knots, upset and **nauseous** to the point I would miss school.

Nowadays, whenever I feel insecure, I find myself doing whatever it takes to make my environment secure, at times controlling those around me. In fact, fear is what frequently fuels a spirit of **control**. For instance, if you see someone micromanaging employees or family members, chances are, their controlling behavior is only the tip of the iceberg — and unseen fear is what lies underneath.

Fear may also lead to **depression**, making it **difficult to sleep or perform everyday tasks**. It can cause us to hide by **isolating ourselves**, make us **unwilling to take risks**, and convince us to **procrastinate**. In fact, my fear of failure has caused me to procrastinate with my writing. Some days, I will do anything — even those things that don't thrill me, like cleaning the house — before I finally plop myself down in front of the computer to write.

 How has fear been fleshed out in your life?

## The Roots and Fruit of Fear

*"So we see that they were not able to
enter, because of their unbelief."*

HEBREWS 3:19

At the root of fear are lies, often based on our misconceptions of God. Misconceptions might include the belief that God is out to get us, that He does not have our best interest at heart, that He is unpredictable and frequently changes His mind, or that He cannot be depended on. When we let such misperceptions of God take root, we lose trust in Him and, instead, place trust in ourselves and our own power. Now thinking we have to fight our battles alone, our hearts become gripped with fear.

Since we start down the slippery slope of fear by believing lies about who God is, it is important to note that the origin of such unhealthy fear is Satan, the father of lies. Fear does not come from God. 2 Timothy 1:7 AKJV says,

"For God hath not given us the spirit of fear; but of power, and of love, and of a sound mind."

Further down the slippery slope, we enter into a cycle: in the same way that misconceptions of God create fear, fear creates further misconceptions about God. It leads us to vain imaginings about the bad things that might happen and encourages us to believe lies from the enemy rather than truth from God's Word. Viewing life and God through a fear lens, we refuse to believe who God says He is and what He promises us in Scripture. It's like we get amnesia, forgetting what God has done and how He's come through for us in the past. We end up doubting God and thinking negatively, which makes us grumble and complain. And we end up being drawn away from God, which keeps us from obeying His will for our lives.

Thus, fear skews our perception of God and reality; slants our belief system, creating further apprehension and anxiety; and prevents us from seeing God's work in our lives. Quite simply, fear keeps us from believing that God is good all the time.

 How has fear distorted your perception of God?

This cycle of fear and distortion of God ultimately results in sin and keeps us from reaching our God-given destiny. As author Bill Johnson, in *When Heaven Invades Earth*, writes, "When I have misconceptions of who He is and what He is like, my faith is restricted by those misconceptions." And we can only go as far as our faith takes us.

Consider the reconnaissance mission in the Promised Land in Numbers 13 and 14. The Lord had instructed Moses to send twelve Israelite spies to explore Canaan, the land God had given to them. When the spies returned from their mission, their report to Moses began favorably; they said the land flowed with milk and honey, and they displayed a sample of the bountiful fruit they had gathered.[67] However, their next words were born out of their fears, as they focused on the huge and powerful people who lived there. Ultimately, it was these fears that persuaded them to refuse to enter Canaan. In fact, the Israelites not only refused to go but they also wept aloud and grumbled against Moses to the point that they thought slavery looked better

than the Promised Land. Their fears had taken over and altered their perception so that they preferred captivity over freedom. They became willing to
disobey God as they submitted to their fears instead of to Him.[68]

But two spies, Caleb and Joshua, were different than the others; they saw
their situation through eyes of faith. They believed the Lord was with them
and would help them fight the Canaanites and conquer them. Joshua and
Caleb knew without a doubt that God could and would lead them into the
land He had promised them.[69]

So God told the ten spies who disbelieved that they would never see the
Promised Land.[70] He went on to say that only Joshua and Caleb would enter.

Like the ten spies whose fear overturned their faith in God, we also face
consequences to our unbelief: if we give into fear the way the ten anxious
spies did, we also will not see our Promised Land. In other words, we can
kiss our destinies good-bye.

> What consequences have you reaped due to
> fear and unbelief? In what way has fear robbed
> you of your God-given destiny? Do you prefer the
> comfort of captivity, or do you want to walk in
> freedom by slamming the door shut to fear?

The good news is that while fear robs us of our destiny, faith releases us
to fulfill it.

## Faith versus Fear

*When I am afraid, I will put my trust in You.*

PSALM 56:3 (NASB)

The antithesis of fear is faith; that is, fear cannot be present when faith
takes the stage. The tenth edition of *Merriam Webster's Collegiate Dictionary* defines faith as "belief and trust in and loyalty to God, a firm belief in
something for which there is no proof," while the description in Hebrews 11:1
exhorts us to go beyond the expression "Seeing is believing" and to believe
without seeing: "Now faith is confidence in what we hope for and assurance

about what we do not see." In short, faith is the absence of unbelief; it is trusting in God, His sovereignty, and His covenant.

Our faith in God is also what makes us steadfast and secure. Oswald Chambers writes, "The great thing about faith in God is that it keeps a man undisturbed in the midst of disturbance." This reminds me of Matthew 8:23–27. The disciples and Jesus got into a boat, and Jesus fell asleep. All of a sudden, a furious storm came upon the lake, but Jesus remained asleep until His frantic disciples woke Him, panicking they would drown. Jesus replied, "You of little faith, why are you so afraid?"[77]

Think of fear and faith as two different sides of a coin. On one side, you see the words "In God We Trust," but on the other side, those words are absent. Like a coin, our lives can show only one side at a time: our faith and belief in God ("In God We Trust") or our fear and disbelief in God. We have the power to choose which side of the coin remains visible in our lives. Read through the list below to see which rules your life more: fear or faith.

| Fear | Faith |
| --- | --- |
| Causes us to hide | Causes us to be transparent |
| Causes us to run in the opposite direction | Causes us to face and embrace fear |
| Immobilizes us | Moves or activates us |
| Tempts us to disobey God | Encourages us to obey God |
| Enslaves and keeps us in captivity | Liberates us |
| Torments us with lies from the enemy | Gives us peace through God's truth |
| Causes us to miss out on God's blessings | Leads us by the hand into our destiny |
| Fuels a spirit of control to gain security | Turns over the situation to God's control |
| Causes procrastination | Hastens us to get it done |
| Robs us of our destinies | Releases us to the purposes of God |

How does fear currently affect your life? Based on the fear-faith chart, which rules your life more: fear or faith?

When we're fearful, it's almost as if we have faith in the very things that we are afraid of or don't want. Many of us have financial fears — that God won't provide enough. We're fearful that something will go wrong with our health and that somehow God isn't capable of taking care of us. We become anxious regarding how our children will mature or whether our spouse will remain faithful. Phobias, such as a fear of heights, fear of flying, fear of snakes, and being claustrophobic, plague us. Anxiety is the fruit of fearful thoughts. Our fears affect our lives spiritually, mentally, emotionally, and physically. When we don't have faith in God and don't let Him rule in our hearts, our fears rule us instead. George Mueller once said, "The beginning of anxiety is the end of faith; the beginning of true faith is the end of anxiety."

Where is your faith: In God or in the wrong thing?

## Fear Be Gone!

*Do not be anxious about anything, but in every situation, by prayer and petition, with thanksgiving, present your requests to God. And the peace of God, which transcends all understanding, will guard your hearts and your minds in Christ Jesus.*

PHILIPPIANS 4:6–7

There are many avenues for fighting fear, and the best route often depends on the situation. However, one of these avenues is required and must be taken before any of the others, and that is to replace the lies you're believing with the truth.

63

## Replace the Lies with Truth

Replacing the lies you believe with truth can stop the fear cycle before it gains a foothold. It requires four main steps:

1. **Identify the lie.** Pinpointing the lie where fear makes its entrance and begins to take root in your heart is the place where you unravel the lie and release the hold of fear. As soon as you feel the first hint of anxiety, ask yourself, "What am I believing about God and the current situation?" Many of us believe the same lie the Israelites believed: *God is not for me; He's against me and doesn't have my best interests at heart.*

2. **Remember who God is.** The presence of God was with the Israelites. He was their front guard and rear guard, guiding and protecting them with the cloud by day and the pillar of fire by night. But fear had made them forget about God's goodness and faithfulness. In your own experience, you can battle such forgetfulness by recalling who God has been in your life. Remember how He's rescued you in the past and will therefore do it again. Spending time in God's Word and reading testimonies about His faithfulness can also help you remember the truth about who He is. God is good and loving; therefore, His actions display His love and goodness toward us. The enemy is relentless with his accusations and lies, but God's love for us is even more relentless.

3. **Replace the lie with the truth.** Now you can substitute the lie you have identified with the truth of who God is. For example, if the Israelites had not missed the opportunity to remember God's faithfulness to them, they could have replaced the lie they believed (*God is not for me; He's against me and doesn't have my best interests at heart*) with the truth: *God is for me; He is with me and wants what is best for me.*

4. **Continue to remind yourself of the truth.** Because the enemy continually hounds us with lies, we need to continually remind ourselves of the truth. For example,

   > I sometimes awake in the middle of the night only to fixate on fearful thoughts. During those times, I discern the lie I'm telling myself that's making me anxious, then I focus on the

corresponding truth I've identified. In fact, I not only remind myself of the truth mentally but I also declare it out loud, so that what's in my mind will drop down to my heart.

Memorizing scriptures that speak to the lies you struggle with can also make this process easier, enabling you to quickly retrieve truth and restore peace in your heart. In my own life, for instance, instead of spiraling out in fear when I believe I can't do something, I remind myself that "I can do all things through Christ who strengthens me."[72] And during the global pandemic, God instructed me to memorize Psalm 91, because He knows my vulnerability toward fear and my need to have His truth hidden in my heart. Another great passage I meditate on is Matthew 6:25–33, where Jesus instructs us to recognize how well He takes care of us in order not to worry.

As for the Israelites, they might have stood on Jeremiah 29:11 to continually reinforce the truth that God had their best interest in mind: "'For I know the plans I have for you,' declares the Lord, 'plans to prosper you and not to harm you, plans to give you hope and a future.'"

> What current situation do you need to apply these four steps to alleviate your fear?

Replacing lies with truth is a prerequisite for combatting fear in other ways, which means that, although it's a necessary step, it's by no means the only one. Additional avenues include facing your fear, drawing closer to Jesus, trusting and obeying God, fearing the Lord rather than man, and starving your fear while feeding your faith.

## Facing Your Fear

Fear controls your life; facing your fear releases freedom. I have had to push through fear my whole life, but God revealed this truth to me in the summer of 2001. I was getting ready to travel to the nation of Syria with

World Vision, and the upcoming trip had brought up a whole new set of fears. It would be my first short-term trip without my spouse, and I would have to travel overseas alone. Although I am half Syrian, neither my mom nor her siblings had ever traveled back to their parents' homeland, so I had no personal knowledge of the area. Not knowing anyone on the team, which was comprised of five different nationalities, caused further apprehension. But it was the prospect of staying alone in the hotels in Syria that scared me the most. Before I left, the Lord gave me this revelation: *When we face our fears, freedom is found.*

The trip to Syria ended up being a dream come true. God divinely orchestrated my seat from Amsterdam to Syria to be next to the team leader. All my teammates were easy to be with, and we had unity in spite of the diverse nationalities. But perhaps the best part was that the thing I feared the most — staying alone in the hotel room — became my biggest blessing. Because my intimacy with the Lord deepened during my times alone with Him at night in my hotel.

Toward the end of the trip, one such night stood out. With earbuds in, I twirled, danced, and sang to worship music. After several minutes of worshiping, I climbed into bed with my journal and pen. Tears began to cascade as I grieved over the thought of leaving my new Syrian friends. With my heart now attached to theirs, I wondered how I would be able to leave them. The Syrian people had stolen my heart!

Tears continued to fall as God's love overwhelmed me. I felt so valued by God and couldn't understand why He loved me with such great depth. I sat still and listened to Him explain how my tears were a form of intercession.

A couple of days after that, we toured an ancient citadel in the northern city of Aleppo. In the middle of one of the rooms, the Muslim tour guide stopped, looked at me, and said, "You're a queen."

Baffled by his pronouncement, I asked him if that's what Norma meant in Arabic.

"No," he replied and then kept going.

As I followed the tour guide and walked toward another room, the Lord whispered in my ear, *That's who I see you as. You're a queen.* For a woman who had struggled with shame and low self-worth, being identified as a queen changed my perception of myself and gave me new confidence.

By the end of the trip, I realized that if I had not faced my fear and taken the trip, my freedom could still be buried. If I had allowed my fears to overpower me, I would have missed hearing God's destiny-speaking voice.

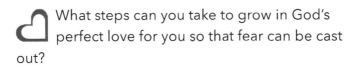 Describe a time when you faced your fear. What were the results?

## Drawing Closer to Jesus

A good way to do away with the fear that constantly nudges you is to get to know God. That's because faith has nothing to do with what you or I can do. Rather, faith is all about what God can do. When I become more intimate with God, I get to know who He is and what He's like. In so doing, I come to know how much He loves me, and I realize He only wants the best for me. Then I am assured that there is nothing to fear. Put more simply, as our intimacy with Jesus deepens and we accurately see God's nature, His love removes our fear. The apostle John, in 1 John 4:18, writes, "There is no fear in love. But perfect love drives out fear… ." And Oswald Chambers, in the June 5 entry of *My Utmost for His Highest*, puts it this way: "The only way to remove the fear from our lives is to listen to God's assurance to us."

What steps can you take to grow in God's perfect love for you so that fear can be cast out?

One of the most direct and immediate examples of this was when John and I went on a Trek Travel bike tour of Banff, Alberta, Canada. On the third day, I woke up with intense anxiety — frightened of descending the winding mountain and cycling fifty miles. So before we left the safety of our hotel room, I prayed and had my husband take authority over the spirit of fear that gripped my heart. My anxiety lessened a bit after that, but it was still there.

Then shortly before I climbed onto my bike, I sat quietly before the Lord. He instructed me to declare His names aloud when I whizzed down the mountain. So as I cycled downhill, I did just that. I proclaimed, "You're my *alpha* and *omega*, my strength and provider. God, you are always with me. You are my healer, protector, and defender." On and on, I declared God's character, and as I did, peace poured into my heart and mind. Drawing near to God and recognizing who He is did away with my fear.

> Which of God's attributes do you need to affirm in order to receive His peace in place of fear?

## Trusting and Obeying God

Even though I have a slight fear of heights, my husband and I decided to go on a canopy tour near Manuel Antonio in Costa Rica. While riding the first of eleven zip lines, I hardly looked down. I grabbed the cable, held on for dear life, and kept my eyes straight ahead on the platform. Gradually, I felt comfortable enough to look around at the beautiful rain forest and even at the river below. I was fine until I got stuck — not once, not twice, but three times! By the third time, I just wanted to be back inside the safe confines of our resort.

I was close to the platform the first time I got stuck, so the guide instructed me to extend my legs, and he pulled me in. The second time, I was a bit farther from the platform. The guide shimmied out toward me, wrapped his legs around mine, and pulled me safely back to the stand. Being even farther out the third time, I came to a complete halt on the zip line. Remembering what the guide had taught us to do, I turned myself around and began pulling myself backward toward the platform, when I saw another guide sailing down the line toward me. I turned around just in time for him to push me onto the platform. Believe me, walking never felt so good!

A few weeks later in the comfort of my home, I was spending time with the Lord, when He asked me if I was still stuck on the zip line.

"No, I'm no longer stuck," I said.

Then He taught me what to do whenever I become stuck in fear: *You always have other options. Not to mention the truth that I am always with you. The three times you were stuck, the guides used three different ways to bring you back home to the platform. You survived, and you thanked them for rescuing you.*

*But you had to trust the guides knew how to save you. You had to not only believe in them but also cooperate with them and do what they asked you to do.*

*Many times in life, you will become fearful and feel stuck. At those times, believe, trust, and obey Me. When you get stuck, believe what your heavenly Instructor is telling you. Trust in what I have to say. I know best, and I have greater knowledge and insight into the situation. Obey Me and you will begin moving again, back toward the security of the platform.*

Whenever we feel stuck and afraid in life, we always have other options. And God will always be able to rescue us from that spot, if only we trust and obey Him.

> In what areas do you feel stuck and afraid, as if there is no way out? Ask God for His options to get you unstuck. How can you show your heavenly Guide that you trust Him to get you unstuck?

Romans 4:18–21 shows us what trust in God looks like through the example of Abraham:

> "Against all hope, Abraham in hope believed and so became the father of many nations, just as it had been said to him, 'So shall your offspring be.'… Yet he did not waver through unbelief regarding the promise of God but was strengthened in his faith and gave glory to God, being *fully persuaded that God had power to do what He had promised* [italics mine]."

When God promised Abraham that Sarah would bear a child and thus make him "the father of many nations," Abraham did not deny that he and Sarah were both old and way past childbearing age. But instead of putting his trust and confidence in the obvious, which would have led to doubt and unbelief, he placed his trust in God — the One who could do what He said He would do. By so doing, Abraham "became the father of many nations."

Smith Wigglesworth says, "Nothing in the world glorifies God so much as simple rest of faith in what God's Word says."

Describe a time when you trusted God. How did you feel and what were the results?

I wonder how many blessings I've missed out on because my fear prevented me from obeying God. It grieves me to think that my disobedience, the product of my fears, robs me and others of God's best.

In what ways has fear caused you to disobey God and miss out on His blessings? How are others negatively affected by your fear?

## Fearing God and Not Man

One of the fears I still struggle with is fear of man. I know all too well the first half of Proverbs 29:25: "Fear of man will prove to be a snare…" When I fear man, I am hesitant to share my opinions. Instead of asserting myself and speaking the truth in love, I run away from confrontation. And I become overly compliant, to the point that I no longer know who I am. I also end up enabling others, which isn't healthy for them or me. I may even end up doing something that I know wouldn't please God. And all of this is because I want to be well liked.

When I need man's acceptance to feel okay about myself, I bow down to the idol of fear of man. Idols are anything or anyone we find comfort in or place our trust in instead of God — which is why our fears are often connected to idols. When we're afraid, we seek comfort and grasp for something to put our trust in. (As another example, I run to food to comfort me when I become afraid, making food an idol as well.) It's no surprise, then, that fear of man is a trap the enemy wants us to fall into.

To override fear of man, we must get to the place where our value and worth comes from one source: God's unconditional love and acceptance. One way to get there is through a healthy fear of the Lord. When I speak of fear in this way, I am not saying we need to see God as an angry dictator who we need to fear because of punishment. Rather, I am talking about the biblical meaning of the fear of the Lord, which Brennan Manning, in *Abba's*

*Child,* defines as "silent wonder, radical amazement and affectionate awe at the infinite goodness of God."

Quite simply, the more reverence we have for God, the less fear we have for man.

 Ask the Holy Spirit to show you if you fear Him more than man.

## Feeding Faith and Starving Fear

As we know, fear is the antithesis of faith. Fear and faith cannot be present at the same time. So by feeding and growing one, we can starve and shrink the other.

One effective way that I feed my faith is to reflect on how God has come through for me in the past. I know if He's done it before, He can surely do it again. Listening to other peoples' testimonies of God's goodness and faithfulness also nourishes my faith. As Revelation 12:11 says, "They overcame ... by the blood of the Lamb and by the word of their testimony."

We can also feed our faith by asking God to help us in our areas of unbelief. Sometimes when fear has snuffed out my faith, I pray, "I do believe; help me overcome my unbelief."[73] Whenever we begin to doubt or fear, we need not hesitate to ask God for more faith — and to have the kind of faith that believes whatever God says *must* be true. That's the kind of prayer the Lord loves to answer.

In the same way that we can feed faith, we can also unwittingly feed fear. When the events of 9/11 occurred, I constantly watched the news and listened to the many dreadful stories being told by victims and witnesses. I finally had to turn off the news so that peace could be restored to my heart. Similarly, we can starve our fear by limiting anything that we are reading, watching, or listening to that may be feeding it.

 What are some practical things you can do to starve your fear?

. . . . . . . . . . . . . . . . . . . . . . . . . . .

## Reframing My Memory of Fear

I walk through the door and discover I'm in the wrong house. Jesus takes my hand and leads me out the front door. I crouch on the floor in the back seat of my mom's car, and Jesus comes over and covers me. He hides me from my enemies and protects me from all harm.

Tears well up. I no longer feel alone or as if I need to protect myself, because God is with me. I know that He is the One who led me out of trouble into a place of safety. He is my covering and my protector. Peace envelopes me, for I am safe with God, and I no longer doubt that He is the One who will take care of me.

## What I Heard My Father Say

*I am with you wherever you go, holding onto your hand. You need not be afraid, for I am here, right by your side. There is absolutely no possibility that I will leave you. I will not let you down. I will always do what I say and be who I am. Therefore, I could never fail you. I am your protector and the One who takes care of you. Trust in Me, and fear no more.*

**Take time to wait before the Lord.**
**Ask Him what He wants to say to you regarding this chapter.**

## ~ The Heart of the Matter ~

- Drawing near to God and recognizing who He is lessens our fear.

- Fear immobilizes us and leads to disobedience.

- Fear prevents us from accurately seeing who God is.

- Fear robs us of our destiny, while faith releases us to fulfill the purposes of God.

- When we face our fears, freedom is found.

- Fear gets stronger when we feed it. Starve what feeds your fear.

- Faith is the opposite of fear.

- When we become fearful, we need to trust and obey God.

- The more reverence we have for God, the less fear we will have of man.

- Our faith is built when we reflect on how God has come through for us in the past.

- God's perfect love for us casts out fear.

— 5 —

# THINKING NOTHING BUT THE TRUTH

*For as he thinks within himself, so he is.*

PROVERBS 23:7A (NASB)

"Oh, God, help me. I don't want to die." Tears blurred my vision. Driving home from church alone, I struggled with the diagnosis I'd received only days earlier. "I'm only twenty-seven, how could I have thyroid cancer? What will happen to my husband?"

My mind raced through scenes of my funeral and my husband with a new bride. In the blink of an eye, I had myself dead and buried and John remarried. I felt desperate.

The Lord confronted me in my thoughts. *Do you know for sure that will happen?*

"No, I don't."

*Tell yourself the truth,* He replied.

It's been over thirty years since that incident, and as you guessed, I didn't die and John didn't remarry. But it clearly shows that whatever we tell ourselves and believe has drastic effects on our emotions and behavior. Proverbs 23:7 (NASB) says, "For as he thinks within himself, so he is." In other words, we become our thoughts. If we believe lies, we will act out of those lies as if they are truth.

We have seen this reality play out again and again throughout the previous four chapters, as we discussed abandonment, rejection, shame, and fear — wounds all rooted in believing lies — which is why I now conclude Part 1 with a chapter on truth-thinking.

God wants us to tell ourselves nothing but the truth, because He knows that doing so is in our best interest. Understanding and believing truth is integral both to our emotional well-being and to our intimacy with others and with Him.

# We Are What We Think

*Do not be deceived: God cannot be*
*mocked. A man reaps what he sows.*

GALATIANS 6:7

No matter how hard we may try, we can't live beyond our thoughts. What we think about and believe, we become. For this reason, we must pay constant, close attention to our thoughts. The following sections, which cover the biblical principle of sowing and reaping, a concept in psychology called the ABCs of Thoughts, and a more practical discussion of judgments and vows, will help you learn to do this.

## Sowing and Reaping

We are sowing seeds in our mind all the time, even when we don't realize it. In the physical world, every seed we plant produces its own kind. If we plant soybeans, we will reap soybeans, not watermelons. Likewise, if we plant seed in our minds to please the Spirit, we will reap peace and eternal life, but if we sow seed to gratify our sinful nature, we will reap destruction.[74] Our minds are the seedbed to what our lives will harvest one day. And each thought we choose to dwell on is a seed we plant for the crop that we will eventually yield.

Crops typically take time, patience, and nurturing, and they bear fruit in a later season; the results are not immediate. But we can know without a doubt that what we've sown in our thoughts will eventually be seen in our lives. Further, seed often yields more than we planted — much like planting my imagined death from thyroid cancer yielded a crop abundant with fear and grief. For all these reasons, we must pay close attention to our thoughts.

Pastor and author Bill Johnson says, "I can't afford to have thoughts in my head that aren't in God's." If we want to reap a harvest of life and peace later, we must choose to sow God's truth in our minds now. If we instead choose to focus on lies from the enemy now, it's like agreeing with him and choosing destruction for our lives later. The negativity on repeat in our heads will whittle away at our identity in Christ, and our "stinking thinking" will yield a harvest of regret.[75]

What we think about and believe, we become. If we want a different life, we need to think different thoughts.

> What kind of thoughts have you sown and what kind of harvest have you reaped accordingly? What different thoughts do you need to think in order to have a different life?

## The ABCs of Thoughts

While getting my master's degree in counseling, I worked with a doctoral student who taught my fourth graders an Adlerian principle he called the ABCs of Thoughts. Its premise, which mirrors the biblical principle of sowing and reaping, is this: people's thoughts about a given experience will influence their emotions and reactions in regard to that experience. Each letter in the abbreviation ABC stands for a specific part of the experience:

- **A** refers to the **Action,** or the situation that you experience. Let's say my husband and I plan a date night. It has been a while since our last one, so we are looking forward to being together. But right before we are to leave for dinner, my husband gets called in to work at the hospital.

- **B** is your **Belief,** or what you tell yourself, about the situation. In the example above, my belief might be, "This is awful! We rarely have time alone together, and now I've been robbed of my date night!" Or I could take a more positive and truthful perspective: "Someone desperately needs my husband right now more than I do, and that is important. Besides, this will give me time to read that new novel I've been wanting to start on. And since he's working tonight, we might be able to go out tomorrow night instead."

- **C** stands for **Consequence.** In this case, the consequence is what we feel and do as a result of the belief we have formed. If I had the first (negative) belief above — that I'd been robbed of my date night — my consequence would be to feel distraught and maybe even shattered. But with the second (positive) belief — that the emergency patient would benefit, that I could finally start my novel, and that we could still likely have a date night the following evening — I would be disappointed but not devastated.

The resulting ABC equation is this:

**A**ction (the experience) +

**B**elief (thoughts about the experience) =

**C**onsequence (feelings and reactions)

The most important part of the equation is always the belief — what we tell ourselves about the events in our life — because that is what determines the outcome. So when I wake up in the middle of the night worried about a situation (A), I can choose one of the following behaviors:

- I can lie in bed thinking about all the things that could go wrong, letting my what-ifs turn into vain imaginations and beliefs (B), thus working myself into an anxious frenzy, unable to fall back asleep (C).
- I can tell myself the truth by recalling scriptures that pertain to the situation, declaring them out loud — "I can do all things through Christ who strengthens me"[76] — (B), thus restoring peace to my heart as I drift off into quiet slumber (C).

Describe a recent experience. What were your beliefs and consequences in that experience? What are some other beliefs you could have had about that experience? How would those alternative beliefs have made you feel, and what might have you done differently as a result?

## Lies, Judgments, and Vows, Oh My!

"You're not a burden, Mom."

Tears sprang to my eyes when my daughter said these words to me over dinner. Her statement had hit the bull's-eye of an unknown wound lodged deep within my heart.

If you're around me long enough, you will hear me say, "I want to be user-friendly." By that I mean that I don't want to rock the boat or require anything from you, and this desire stems from a couple of things: First, I want to receive others' acceptance and to avoid rejection and loneliness. And second, I don't want to be a burden to others.

Later that evening, the Lord revealed to me a memory of the exact moment through which feeling like a burden had entered my heart and mind. I was nine years old, and anger spewed from my dentist's mouth: "Why did you make your extraction appointment today? This is the day my favorite team is playing in the World Series. I'd rather be home watching the game!"

*This must be all my fault,* I thought. *I hate being a burden. From now on, I won't require anything from anyone. I'll be user-friendly so that I can gain acceptance.* As that nine year old, I made the judgment that I was a burden, and as a result, I unconsciously promised myself I would no longer require anything from anyone. To this day, it is difficult to ask someone a favor because I don't want to be an incumbrance.

My fear of facing rejection over being a bother all began with a lie I believed, which led to my making a judgment and then a vow. If you remember from chapter 2, a judgment is a life concept we form based on an event, and a vow is a generalized decision about how to live based on that event. More specifically, vows are promises we make to ourselves, either knowingly or unknowingly, to live in a certain way that we think will prevent future hurt. Sometimes judgments, and the vows that stem from them, come as the result of several events added up together.[1]

So what's the problem with judgments? Whenever we make a judgment about a person, we shut down a segment of our trust in both that person and

---

1  Note that a judgment is different from a belief (as defined in the ABCs of Thoughts). A belief is tied to the specific event, whereas a judgment is an idea about "life in general" that can spring from one event or a collection of events. Likewise, a consequence differs from a vow in that a consequence is a result or reaction tied directly to the event from which it sprang, whereas a vow is a generalized decision about how to live life in the future.

in people in general. It's like we close the door of our heart to a certain part of having relationships with them. As a result, we will become less open to opportunities to grow in those relationships. For instance, let's say a close friend betrays me and I make the judgment, "No one can be trusted. All close friendships will eventually turn on me." As a result of this judgment, I will become less open than before to forming close friendships with others.

Another problem with making a judgment is that it puts me in the position of judge, but God is the only one with the right or authority to that position. In fact, Jesus directly commands us not to judge: "Do not judge, or you too will be judged. For in the same way you judge others, you will be judged, and with the measure you use, it will be measured to you."[77] What this verse is saying is that when we pass judgment on others, in essence, we condemn ourselves. I've noticed that I also tend to judge others in the same areas I'm most critical about in myself. It's as if I mentally point out their sins as a way to distract myself from seeing and dealing with my own sin.

The problem with vows is also that they place us in the driver's seat, controlling the situation, instead of sitting in the back seat, allowing God to be in control. If you remember, typical vows are "I will" statements: "I will never trust anyone. I will never allow someone to become close to me." As such, vows also encourage us to close ourselves off from relationships and opportunities for growth.

Judgments and vows become strongholds that rule our lives, dictating where we'll go. But they start out by simply agreeing with a lie. To remove our judgments and vows so that our hearts can be healed, we need to confess them to God and seek His forgiveness, identify and renounce the lies that started them, pull the root of misbelief out of our mind and heart, and replace it with a new seed of truth. Then we will be free from their control.

In my own experience, I replaced the lie "I'm a burden" with the truth "I'm a blessing."

> Ask the Holy Spirit to reveal to you any lies you've believed that have turned into judgments and vows. Repent of those and replace them with truth to form a new operating system to govern your life.

# Choosing Truth Over Deception

*He was a murderer from the beginning, not holding to*
*the truth, for there is no truth in him.*
*When he lies, he speaks his native language,*
*for he is a liar and the father of lies.*

JOHN 8:44B

What we tell ourselves determines the condition of our life, which is why establishing right thoughts is so important. The first step toward having right thoughts is to discern deception, and the second is to learn how to demolish it. Only then can we begin to change our mind and the course of our life.

## Discern the Deception

Author Nancy Leigh DeMoss, in *Lies Women Believe,* says "the root of most of our struggles is: You and I have been lied to. We have been deceived." She goes on to say that "the 'best' lies are those that look the most like the truth" — which is why deceitful thoughts from the enemy are so hard to detect and easy to believe. Perhaps worse, deception is sometimes like bad breath — you're the last one to know you've gotten it.

So how can we figure out when we're being deceived? My pastor used to say "Make your thoughts show their ID." In other words, ask who the author of your thoughts is. Are your beliefs from God, Satan, or your flesh? Ask the Holy Spirit to show you when you've been misled by the enemy. Also ask Him to help you discern the lies you've already believed and to know and believe the truth.

Our enemy likes to deceive and mislead us, just as he did with Adam and Eve.[78] He wants us to disbelieve what is true, so he can gain ground in our thoughts and control us. In fact, the name Satan means "the adversary." The Bible calls Satan by other names that reveal his character too. For instance, devil means "slanderous," because his intent is to insult God's character as well as ours. He's also known as the tempter, the accuser, and the father of lies.

Conversely, Jesus described Himself as "the way and *the truth* and the life."[79] And Priscilla Shirer, in *The Armor of God,* defines truth as "God's opinion on any matter." Quite simply, when we get to know God, we get to know truth. We do this by spending time with Him in prayer and in His Word.

In the same way that bank tellers are trained to recognize counterfeit bills by studying real money, we must train to distinguish lies from the truth by studying God's Word. Reading the Bible daily and memorizing Scripture is like turning on the light in a dark room: it exposes what was hidden in darkness.

> Whose voice do you most often listen to: God's, the enemy's, or your own?

## Condemnation or Conviction?

One way to discern where a belief comes from and whether it is a truth or a lie is to determine whether it makes you feel condemned or convicted. Condemnation is defined as "to judge, to pronounce sentence against, to disapprove, to blame." Conviction, on the other hand, means "to convince of sin, to prove or determine to be guilty." While the Holy Spirit shines His light on our sin through conviction, God never condemns us. Romans 8:1 says, "Therefore, there is now no condemnation for those who are in Christ Jesus." The Bible also tells us that Jesus came not to condemn the world but to save it.[80]

One way to evaluate whether you're feeling convicted or condemned is to ask yourself what you are focusing on. Conviction's attention is on your relationship with Jesus while condemnation highlights you. The enemy's goal is that we focus on feeling bad about ourselves while our Lord desires restoration in our hearts and in our relationship with Him.

The table that follows sheds more light on the difference between conviction and condemnation.

| Conviction | Condemnation |
|---|---|
| The Holy Spirit is the author.[81] | Satan, the enemy, is the accuser.[82] |
| It targets a specific sin. | It is general and vague. You're unable to pinpoint the exact wrong that you've done. |
| It brings life and freedom.[83] | It brings death, destruction, and captivity. |
| It comes by way of a gentle voice. | It comes by way of a harsh and overwhelming voice. |
| You feel hopeful, cleansed, and forgiven.[84] | You feel hopeless, slimed, and ashamed. |
| It draws you toward God as you repent and receive God's forgiveness. | It draws you away from God because you feel the problem is too big to be forgiven and you're unworthy to receive God's forgiveness. |
| It attacks your sinful action. | It attacks your character — the core of who you are. |
| The end result is that your relationship with God is restored and you find peace. | The end result is that you beat yourself up emotionally and are miserable. |

When my kids were elementary age, I struggled with anger and yelling. The enemy would taunt me with, *You're a lousy mom! You'll never have self-control,* and then sarcastically whisper, *You really represented God to your kids.* I'd walk away disheartened.

Later I learned that this was condemnation and deceit from the enemy, and I learned to listen to God's voice more closely. He would gently instruct me, *You sinned when you yelled at your kids. Go and ask them to forgive you.* I'd confess my sins of anger and yelling, and He would faithfully forgive me and purify my unrighteousness.[85]

God's grace always encourages us, affirms our character, and picks us up when we stumble.

Describe examples of conviction and condemnation in your own life. How did they affect you differently?

## Demolish Deception by Declaring Truth

Once you have discerned deception, you can take steps to demolish it.

In his book *Soul Care,* Dr. Rob Reimer writes, "The power of a lie is in our agreement with it. Whatever we agree with, we give power to." In other words, the lie isn't the problem; our agreement with the lie is. Take, for example, the lie "I am not worthy." That lie, in and of itself, has no hold on me. Only when I agree with the lie and say, "Yes, this is true," does the lie begin to dictate my behavior and control my life — because it is then that I begin to build a stronghold.

In the Old Testament, a stronghold was a secured, protected dwelling built to defend outside attacks. We build strongholds in our heart and mind when we repeatedly agree with and believe Satan's lies. Each lie we agree with is like a brick that we add to our stronghold, fortifying the fortress walls and making them less penetrable for God's truth.

In the previous chapter, I discussed how I've struggled with the stronghold of the fear of man. It manifests itself when I'm hesitant to share my opinions or want to run from confrontation. I become overly compliant to the point that I'm not true to myself and I'm disobedient to God. The lies I've believed, such as "I need the approval of man" or "What others think about me and their acceptance of me is important," are the thought bricks that have added up to build this fortified place in my mind.

To get rid of the lies and let in God's truth, I need to demolish this stronghold. To demolish means to "tear or pull down." In 2 Corinthians 10:4–5, we read the following:

> The weapons we fight with are not the weapons of the
> world. On the contrary, they have divine power to demolish
> strongholds. We demolish arguments and every pretension
> that sets itself up against the knowledge of God, and we take
> captive every thought to make it obedient to Christ.

To demolish the stronghold in my heart and mind, I am to cast down all arguments, speculations, what-ifs, if-onlys, and other thoughts unsupported by Scripture, so that the truth can be erected in its place. I must make the lies I believe bow down to God's truth and Lordship. And I must demolish my stronghold of lies with the Word of God.[86]

Every time I hurl God's truth at my fortress of lies, the stronghold weakens. Each truth I catapult toward it begins to chip away at the bricks, eventually putting holes in the walls and making it weak enough that it can no longer stand. And when it falls, as John 8:32 states, "Then you will know the truth, and the truth will set you free."

For me, when I want to demolish the stronghold of the fear of man, I fling the truths, "I have God's unconditional love and acceptance" and "It's God's opinion and approval of me that counts the most." By thinking on these truths and declaring them out loud, brick by brick, I dismantle the lies I've come to believe with God's infallible truth.

But I do a couple of additional things, as well, to help me bring down my fortress. First, because I have found that unspoken lies remain hidden and only grow larger, I share them with someone I trust who also trusts the Lord, so they can help me see the truth. Second, I get out a pen and a piece of paper. I draw a line vertically down the center to create two columns. In the left column, I write the lies I'm believing. Then in the right column, next to each lie, I write the corresponding truth with a supporting scripture verse. Here's an example:

| Lie | Truth |
| --- | --- |
| I am rejected and worthless. | I am accepted in the Beloved and chosen by God.[87] |
| I'm a victim. | I am victorious in Christ.[88] |
| No one loves me. | God loves me so much that He sent His only Son, Jesus, to die for me.[89] |
| I'm stupid. | I have the mind of Christ.[90] |
| I can't do anything right. | I can do all things through Christ.[91] |
| My sins are too great to be forgiven. | I am redeemed and forgiven of all my sins.[92] |

Finally, I renounce each lie and declare the truth.

Speaking Scripture out loud and declaring its truth in the face of a lie not only supports the demolition process but also begins to create and solidify within us a new stronghold — a fortress of belief in the truth, behind which we can stand firm against the enemy and resist temptation.

Declarations help me to intentionally focus on the truth: who God is and what His Word says about me. And by affirming aloud who I am in Christ, I can walk in my God-given authority as His daughter. This builds my faith and increases my expectations of the goodness of God. As Romans 10:17 says, "Consequently, faith comes from hearing the message, and the message is heard through the word about Christ."[93]

> Ask God what lies you believe and write them down. Write the truths next to the lies and add supportive Scripture. Declare these truths aloud.

## Continue to Dwell on the Truth

Declaring the truth from God's Word helps us demolish deception and withstand the onslaught of the enemy. Jesus Himself, as His defense against Satan in the wilderness, said, "It is written…" and then went on to quote the Word of God.[94] To be effective, however, declaring the truth is not an event we can do only once.

Like a recording on repeat in our heads, the lies we've believed have played over and over again, creating a mindset. For a lot of us, those recordings were made by significant people during our formative years, which means they have been playing for many, many years. Developing a new mindset of truth, therefore, is also a process. Romans 12:2a says, "Do not conform to the pattern of this world, but be transformed by the renewing of your mind." We must do this by also pushing the "repeat" button, playing the truth constantly in our thoughts. After doing this for a long enough time, eventually the truth will become our mind's default option.

Throughout my writing journey, I've had to combat the lie that I am incapable by declaring truth out loud over and over again. I look at myself in the mirror and say, "Norma, you are creative. The Creator lives within you." The more often I declare, believe, and agree with this truth, the more my actions align themselves with reality.

What truths do you need to dwell on and declare out loud?

. . . . . . . . . . . . . . . . . . . . . . . . . . . . . .

## Reframing My Memory of Deception

The Lord sits next to me in the passenger seat as I drive home from church. As He watches tears roll down my face, He instructs me to pull the car over. I do as He requests. He takes my face in His hands and says, "My daughter, do not become distraught over the lies you're telling yourself that may not even take place. Instead, tell yourself the truth: I will never leave you." At the sound of His voice and the gentle touch of His hand, peace envelops me. I know that, no matter what happens, everything will be okay.

## What I Heard My Father Say

*My beloved child, tell yourself the truth. Take time to evaluate your emotions and actions based on what you're believing. Recognize the lies you've believed and counteract them by declaring aloud the truth I've given to you in my Word. Understand the difference between conviction and condemnation, and remember I am not the author of condemnation. Just as Scripture says, your thoughts lead you to become who you are. Transformation begins by renewing your mind.*

**Take time to wait before the Lord.**
**Ask Him what He wants to say to you regarding this chapter.**

## ~ The Heart of the Matter ~

- We reap what we sow in our thought life.
- If we want a different life, we need to think different thoughts.
- The broken records of negativity whittle away at our identity in Christ.
- We will become what we think about, agree with, and believe.
- What we believe about events dictates our emotions and actions.
- God's conviction is gentle and specific, while Satan's condemnation is harsh and overgeneralized, attacking our character.
- Judgments and vows are unhealthy responses to the hurts we experience and the lies we believe as a result. Healing comes through renouncing the lies and announcing God's truth.
- We demolish our deception as we replace each lie in our stronghold with God's truth.
- Declarations build faith and increase our expectations of God's goodness.
- Developing a new mindset and renewing our minds is a process that takes time. It's not an event we do only once.
- One way we can distinguish lies from truth is by being a student of God's Word.

# PART 2:
# DEEPENING INTIMACY

My passion for emotional healing is second only to my passion for becoming more intimate with God and others. When I was in fourth grade, for example, I signed all my classmates' Valentine's Day cards, "Love, Norma." I was later mercilessly teased for that sentiment, but I had done it because I wanted everyone to feel and know they were loved and valued. Likewise, God wants each of us to feel and know how loved and valued we are by Him. He created us to find the deepest form of intimacy through our relationship with Him and then, as an outpouring of that closeness, to find intimacy with others.

As such, the second half of this book includes concepts and practices that have helped me draw nearer to God and deepen my intimacy with Him; these include knowing God, which leads to trusting, loving, and obeying Him and to becoming fully alive in our identity. I then conclude the section with two practical tools on how to experience God's presence: "soaking" and listening to His voice.

As you read through the following chapters, I pray that you will enjoy the adventure of deepening your relationship with God and that Psalm 16:11 resonates within your heart: "You have made known to me the path of life; you will fill me with joy in your presence, with eternal pleasures at your right hand."

# — 6 —
# KNOWING GOD

*But whatever were gains to me I now consider
loss for the sake of Christ. What is more,
I consider everything a loss because of the
surpassing worth of knowing Christ Jesus my
Lord, for whose sake I have lost all things. I
consider them garbage, that I may gain Christ.*

PHILIPPIANS 3:7–8

By age seventeen, I had known the Lord for a few years but didn't understand the concept of Lordship. Thus, I had dated a Jewish man, a Mormon, and an agnostic in that short time. Not until I was preparing for my freshman year at the University of Arizona did I promise God I would date only Christians. Then, through a fluke, I was invited to a Sigma Phi Epsilon fraternity rush party. I called my sister Janet, who had dated a few men in that fraternity, and asked, "What are my chances of meeting a Christian at the Sig Ep fraternity?"

"Better there than at most," she replied.

When Janet, my roommate Ann, and I arrived at the party, my husband-to-be happened to be the greeter at the door. Janet had met John the year before while studying in the medical school library, and since I was Janet's little sister, John thought of me as harmless.

Two days later, Ann and I went to the mall and saw John with a friend of his. We said hi, after which I ran into JC Penney's, fell to my knees, and squealed with excitement.

The following weekend, John took me out on a date. And by our tenth day of knowing each other, John had said, "I love you."

"You're just infatuated with me" was my response. "What if I don't fall in love with you? I don't want to hurt you."

"Time will tell," John said. That was the first of numerous times over the past forty years that he's been right!

Those initial months of our relationship were a time of discovery as we mined the depths of each other's hearts. We would try to study together, but it was hopeless, because we couldn't stop asking each other questions in our desire to get closer. I wanted to be with John every spare moment and couldn't get enough time with him.

I can get to know God in the same way — by spending time and communicating with Him. If I could encourage you to have one pursuit in life, it would be this: study His Word and seek to experience Him in daily life. Because, to echo the apostle Paul's admonition in Philippians 3:7–8, *nothing* compares with knowing God.

If you are a Christian, reflect back on when you first met Jesus.

Noah Webster's 1828 dictionary defines *know* as "To perceive with certainty; to understand clearly, to have a clear and certain perception of truth, fact, or anything that actually exists. To know a thing precludes all doubt or uncertainty of its existence." Knowing God in this way is a never-ending pursuit. God's nature is so vast and incomprehensive, it seems that the more I know Him, the less I really know. There is always more to learn about Him. In the same way that I'm still making discoveries of the various facets of my spouse, I will never exhaust mining the truths about my infinite God.

Knowing God in this way also means more than just knowing *about* Him; rather, we must know God personally — we must *experience* Him. There's a difference. I know about the president of the United States, for example, but I don't know him experientially. I have never met him, spent time with him, or communicated with him. On the other hand, I do experientially know my husband, including how he thinks and feels, because I have spent years with him. To know God experientially means being able to say to Him, the way Job did as a result of his suffering, "My ears had heard of you but now my eyes have seen you."[95] We must go beyond head knowledge — beyond knowing facts — to have heart revelation.

How can you increase your heart revelation of who God is since so much weighs upon that one pursuit?

# Trust and Intimacy

*Those who know your name trust in you.*

PSALM 9:10A

We usually don't open up to people we've just met, sharing the most intimate parts of our heart. That's because we don't know them well enough to tell whether they would keep what we share in confidence. Instead, we wait and get to know people so we can gauge their characters. Over time, if we come to believe they're trustworthy, we feel free to share and entrust our heart with them. It's the same way with God. We have to get to know Him, His character, and His nature before we are free to trust Him.

The correlation between trust and intimacy goes the other way around too: the more we trust people, the closer to them we feel. In fact, it's impossible to become closer to someone we *don't* trust.

Trust is the foundation upon which all relationships are built. For this reason, our relationship with God will not grow beyond our level of trust in Him. Author Steve Backlund writes, "Our 'measure of faith,' will increase in proportion to the revelation we have of Gods' character, His love, and His promises toward us." In other words, the more we know God, the more we trust God. And the more we trust God, the closer we become with Him.

Becoming a believer who is "all in" and has developed wholehearted devotion to God is — like many things in life — a progression: when we **know** God, we can't help but **trust** and **love** God. And when we trust and love God, we can't help but **obey** Him. Further, the more we trust and obey God, the more we get to know Him, and the cycle of wholehearted devotion repeats itself, again and again.

 How deep is your trust level of God?

# Perception is Everything

*I am the good shepherd; I know my*
*sheep and my sheep know me.*

JOHN 10:14

In relationships, perception matters. Our perception of someone — or what we believe about that person — affects how we relate to him. If our perception of our parent is that he is harsh and critical and unsafe, we will most likely distrust him, relate to him in fear, and keep our heart closed to him. On the other hand, if we see our parent as loving and supportive, as one who corrects and disciplines us out of love, we will trust him enough to share our innermost dreams and desires with him.

It's the same with our relationship with God the Father. Our perceptions matter! Consider "the top-button theology." The speaker at a women's retreat I attended once demonstrated this idea using a cardigan. When the top button of the sweater was fastened correctly into its corresponding hole, all the buttons below it also aligned properly. But when the top button was fastened into the wrong hole, the rest of the buttons were eschewed. In our walk with God, the top button is the perception "God is good." When we realize, like the psalmist in Psalm 27:13, that "I remain confident of this: I will see the goodness of the Lord in the land of the living," then everything else in life lines up.

We see this same idea of perception played out in the parable of the lost son in Luke 15:11–32. In this story, there is a father with two sons. The younger son leaves home, takes his inheritance with him, and squanders it on wild living. But when he comes to the end of himself, he returns to his father, asking his dad to hire him as a servant. His dad, however, is so thrilled with his son's return that, he throws a party to celebrate. The oldest son responds in anger and refuses to join the festivities. The father entreats him, but the elder son answers, "Look! All these years I've been slaving for you and never disobeyed your orders. Yet you never gave me even a young goat so I could celebrate with my friends."[96]

The elder son's anger was the result of his wrong perception of his father and their relationship. He inaccurately saw his dad as more of a master than a father, and he saw himself as more of slave than a son. He had missed seeing the truth of the father-son relationship. The older son's perception of his dad here is crucial because it's what caused him to respond in such a way that he distanced himself from his dad and brother. Likewise, our perception of God is everything, because it determines the closeness of our relationship with Him.

## Misperceptions about God

Our perception of who God is has a profound impact on how we see ourselves; accuracy in our perception of God breeds accuracy in our perception of ourselves. Jennifer Rothschild, in her Bible study on the book of Hosea, writes, "When you don't have an intimate knowledge of who God is, then you misunderstand Him and misunderstand who you are and what you have." She goes on to say, "When I lack knowledge of God, my sense of identity and value is destroyed. When I don't know who God really is, I have no idea who I am." In other words, accurate and intimate knowledge of God results in accurate and intimate knowledge of who we are and who God created us to be.

A line in Pastor Bill Johnson's *When Heaven Invades Earth* builds on this idea: "We lack understanding of who we are because we have little revelation of who He is." When we see who God is, we begin to see ourselves through His eyes, which is how our identity in Christ, as His child, is formed.

> Do you simply know about God, or do you know Him personally and experientially? How has your knowledge of Him affected your identity?

Equally important, the lens we perceive God through also shapes how we reflect God to others. When we have an accurate picture of who God is, we can accurately portray Him to the world around us. Said another way, when we get to know God better, we can make Him better known.

💙 What do your actions tell the world around you in regard to what you believe about God? Do your thoughts, words, and deeds display trust and intimacy with God, or do they proclaim He is not trustworthy?

It's no wonder our enemy will do anything and everything to prevent us from not only knowing God but also knowing Him accurately — by doing so, he can make us less sure of God, less sure of ourselves, and less effective for God's kingdom.

There are many ways that Satan will try to twist and distort our view of God's character. In the Garden of Eden, he planted doubt in Eve's mind by asking, "Did God really say, 'You must not eat from any tree in the garden'?"[97] Entertaining this doubt led Eve to question God's goodness, which led her to sin against God and separate herself from Him. Today, the deceiver attempts to do the same with us, planting doubt in our minds about what God has said and promised to us in His Word. Our adversary knows that understanding God's goodness allows us to love, trust, and obey Him. By throwing doubt at that understanding, he can misalign the top button "God is good," keep us distant from God, and keep the other important areas of our life from "lining up." If the enemy accomplishes that, he's got us right where he wants us.

💙 Ask the Lord about any distorted perceptions you may have of Him.

Another way that the enemy can cloud our perceptions of God the Father is through our experience with our earthly dad or another male authority figure. By now, I have a long history with God that has given me a realistic view of Him, and as a result, I trust Him with my whole heart. But it hasn't always been that way. I had to do a lot of work to process the hurt from my dad and forgive him before I could keep my view of Father God clear and accurate.

Later in life — in 2016, to be exact — I became ever so grateful that I had made amends with my dad and that God had redeemed the hurt from our relationship. If I hadn't, I most likely would have turned my back on God, or at least would have kept a safe distance, when I was diagnosed with endometrial cancer. I likely would have believed God was against me and wanted to hurt me through the disease. Instead, as I got into my car after getting the diagnosis at the doctor's appointment, through tears, I began to thank God. "Game on," I told Him, and then prayed, "Lord, I give this to you. May you, Jesus, spill over. I embrace this journey and am so grateful you are my traveling companion. Help me, Holy Spirit, to fulfill all that you have for me in this next season."

I desired to give God honor in all that I would say and do during my cancer journey. I wanted Him to know I trusted Him, and I hoped He would be glorified through my obedient submission. I longed to look more like my heavenly Daddy and have His character rub off on me as I pressed myself close to Him and leaned on His strength. I knew God's goodness, believed He had my best interest at heart, and knew He works all things out for the good of those who love Him.[98]

## Truths about God

In the months following my diagnosis, I was able to allow my experience with cancer to deepen my relationship with God and to demonstrate all the more who God is. He's my **comforter** when I'm down and frustrated at my lack of energy. He's my **counselor** and **encourager** when my heart struggles. He's my **companion** when loneliness tries to set in. And He's my **confidant** to whom I pour out my heart to and in whom place my trust.

This experience showed me that our circumstances or outcomes don't determine the truth of who God is. It's easier to say God is good when our outcome or circumstances are good. But it's equally true that God is good when the outcome or circumstances look bad. In reality, God cannot *not* be good, no matter how things go, because it's His nature to be good. He can't be anything but good. In fact, sometimes it's the not-so-good situations that best display the goodness of God. His goodness shines the brightest in the dark.

Which areas in your life are the most difficult to trust God in?

Let's look at some unchanging truths about who God is by exploring His distinctive names and attributes, as outlined in Scripture.

For starters, the Word says God is our **redeemer** and is **compassionate**.[99] He's our **companion** and **friend**.[100] Our Father is also **all-knowing**[101] and **present everywhere**. He's our **rock**,[102] the one who gives stability in the storms of life. And we serve a **holy** God, one who is **unchanging**[103] and **faithful** to keep His covenant.[104]

God is also described as Father, Son, and Holy Spirit, all of whom, together, make up the Trinity. They are all God, but in different forms, based on the roles they play. It is similar to the way H2o is the same compound, whether in the form of water, steam, or ice, or to the way I am one being but wear different hats: daughter, wife, mom, friend, writer, and speaker. Likewise, God the Father, Son, and Holy Spirit display the different facets that make up our beautiful God.

## God the Father

God the Father is my **protector**. He's the one who fights my battles: "Do not be afraid or discouraged because of this vast army. For the battle is not yours, but God's."[105] This aspect of God reminds me of the memory I described earlier, when I would sit on the floor close to my dad's feet while watching a scary TV show. I figured he would protect me if trouble came. I'd cover my face and periodically spread my fingers apart to peek through them. Likewise, when fear and anxiety begin to creep into my heart now, I scoot close to my heavenly Father, knowing He'll protect me.

My heavenly Father is also my **provider**. He takes care of me and provides for all my needs — like the time my husband's patient load plummeted at work and God provided another job. Matthew 6:25–26 reinforces this aspect of God:

> Therefore I tell you, do not worry about your life, what you will eat or drink; or about your body, what you will wear. Is not life more than food, and the body more than clothes? Look at the birds of the air; they do not sow or reap or store away in barns, and yet your heavenly Father feeds them. Are you not much more valuable than they?

In addition, God is **sovereign,** even when the world seems to be falling apart. Everything and everyone are under God's control: "See, the Sovereign Lord comes with power, and he rules with a mighty arm."[106]

**Almighty** is one of my favorite names of God. Jeremiah 32:17 declares that nothing is too hard for God; after all, He created the heavens and the earth. And when I struggle with loneliness, one of God's sweetest names that comforts me in this area is **Immanuel — God with us**. He promises us in Hebrews 13:5 that He will never leave us or forsake us. I can know that I'm never alone, because He's always by my side.

Finally, I clearly witnessed God's attributes of **mercy** and **kindness** when my father's eyes of understanding were opened to grasp the truths of salvation at the age of eighty. God led my dad to repentance, which gave him the gift of salvation and a new spiritual life as his physical life diminished.

 How have you experienced God the Father?

### God the Son, Jesus Christ

I am the bride of Christ; therefore, Jesus is my **Bridegroom,** who rejoices over me.[107] He is the **Lover of my soul**, the one who is passionate about me, and He woos us with words such as, "Arise, my darling, my beautiful one, and come with me."[108] It follows, then, that Jesus is also our **heavenly Husband**. We are not His slave but His spouse. He wants us to call Him husband, not master.[109]

Finally, Jesus is our **Rescuer.** I experienced this poignantly one Christmas morning as our family, along with our son's fiancé, sat in our pajamas and robes, listening to John read the Christmas story in Luke 2. This time, he read it in The Passion translation. When he got to verse 11, I did everything I could to keep the tears from running loose: "For today in Bethlehem a rescuer was born for you. He is the Lord Yahweh, the Messiah." The tears ran their course anyway. You see, we had just experienced God as our rescuer in our move to Wichita. In our previous city, we had been in circumstances beyond our control and had needed someone to intervene — and God did that on our behalf. Jesus truly rescued us, saving us from a difficult situation.

♡ In what ways has God the Son, Jesus Christ,
been manifested in your life?

*God the Holy Spirit*

John's final year of medical training in Chicago was difficult for me, and the Holy Spirit became my **counselor** during that time, as I poured out my heart to Him. (I filled up six journals!) He became my **confidant**, the one who heard about the good, the bad, and the ugly sides of Norma. These characteristics of the Holy Spirit are affirmed in Scripture as well: "But the Advocate, the Holy Spirit, whom the Father will send in my name, will teach you all things and will remind you of everything I have said to you."[110]

In addition, God cares when there is a breach in our relationship with Him — so much so that the Holy Spirit **convicts** us of our sin.[111] He gives us a way to restore our relationship through repentance. Along this same line, He's also known as the **Spirit of truth**: "But when he, the Spirit of truth, comes, he will guide you into all truth. He will not speak on his own; he will speak only what he hears, and he will tell you what is yet to come."[112] When I ask God questions, the Holy Spirit whispers the answers.

I'm grateful the Holy Spirit is also my **intercessor**, one who prays on my behalf. Romans 8:27 says, "And He who searches our hearts knows the mind of the Spirit, because the Spirit intercedes for God's people in accordance with the will of God."

♡ What role does God the Holy Spirit play in
your daily life? Who is God to you? Which of
His character traits are most meaningful to you?

In Jeremiah 9:24, God gives us permission to boast in knowing Him. Knowing the truth about God and His various names is a good start to combatting our misperceptions, but we must also pursue God Himself so that we can come to know these truths experientially, ultimately deepening our trust in and intimacy with Him.

# In Hot Pursuit

*I love those who love me, and those*
*who seek me find me.*

PROVERBS 8:17

As a little girl, one of my favorite games to play at recess was tag, or chase. The person who was "it" would chase everyone else. If you got caught, you became "it" and would chase after the others. For some reason, whenever a boy chased after me, I would let him catch me. God is the same way. He likes to be chased, pursued, and sought after, and when we do that, He lets us catch Him. But God also pursues us and initiates relationship with us. So stop running and let God catch you!

## How God Pursues Us

To pursue means "to follow, to go after, to seek, to endeavor to attain, to strive, reach or gain." One way God pursues each of us is through His acts of kindness.[113] God answering my prayers is an example of how He's in hot pursuit of me, like when He'd find parking spaces near our Chicago brownstone when our kids were two and four years old. Reminding me of His presence by discovering coins laying on the ground is another way He displays His tenderness toward me. Running into a friend unexpectedly and watching His hand orchestrate things with impeccable timing are other avenues His kindheartedness toward me is seen. God is involved in every detail of our lives.

The Holy Spirit's gentle conviction of sin to lead us to repentance is an act of His relentless love pursuit because He is a husband who wants His bride to be in right relationship with Him. When I have offended John and there is a breach in our relationship, I need to repent of my sin to God and ask John for forgiveness. The closest relationships are those without gaps or areas of brokenness because of offense, and that also includes ours with God.

We let God catch us when we go to Him in repentance, when we sit still to listen to His voice, and when we obey what He's asked us to do. Ultimately, what God is after is our heart, and when we surrender that to Him, we've allowed Him to catch us.

## How We Pursue God

The healthiest relationships are those that go two ways — those where both parties equally make the relationship a priority, spending time investing in it to become closer. I don't know about you, but I'd prefer to not be the only one initiating time together with a friend. It would send me the message that they just weren't that interested in the relationship. In the same way, our pursuit of God and our relationship with Him is vital because it shows Him that we love and value Him.

One of the best ways to pursue God is by spending time with Him on a consistent basis. In the same way that my relationship with my husband or friends cannot be close if I rarely spend time with them, my relationship with God cannot be intimate if I spend more time watching TV, browsing Facebook, reading novels, shopping, exercising, or talking on the phone than I spend with God.

Another way to chase after God is through communication — and by *communication*, I mean a two-way conversation. Just like only talking to John and not taking the time to listen to his heart would thwart our connection to each other, monopolizing all my time with God by asking for things in prayer can create distance in my relationship with Him. Sitting still and being intentional in listening to His voice is also necessary to build a close relationship. In my experience, although I spend time in God's Word and pray daily, listening to God's voice and journaling what He says has had the most profound effect on my intimacy with Him. (I elaborate more on the subject of hearing God's voice in the last chapter.)

Our commitment to God is yet another avenue by which we can show our pursuit of Him. All relationships require commitment and faithfulness in order to thrive. In our relationship with God, we can show our commitment in several ways. We can pray consistently, in good times and bad, to show that we are not simply God's "fair-weather" friend. We can make sure not to compartmentalize God by inviting Him only to church or Bible study but to be with Him wherever we go — including the grocery store, doctor's office, classroom, or work. For Christians, there is no separation of sacred and secular; God wants to be involved in whatever we do! Finally, we can show God our commitment by not only including Him in every part of life but also making Him the center. In other words, the Lord doesn't revolve around my work, ministry, relationships, or hobbies. Rather, each of them revolves around Him. He's the hub, and my other areas of interest are the spokes in the wheel. Author Mark Batterson, in his book *All In*, puts it this way: "If Jesus is not Lord of all, then Jesus is not Lord at all. We exist for one reason and one reason alone: to glorify God, and to enjoy him forever."

> How do you pursue the heart of God? How do you involve Him in all aspects of your life? What areas do you still need to surrender to His Lordship?

## Adversity and Pursuit

God loves to do life with each of us. He wants to be personally involved in our adversities and celebrations, mountaintops and valleys, and every moment in between. But when we have trials, He can use them to draw us closer to Him. In fact, it seems my relationship with God grows by leaps and bounds whenever life is hard. Trials, more than triumphs, help me get to know God better. Perhaps, it's because desperation causes me to pursue Him. And as I lean and depend upon Him and see Him answer prayer and part my personal Red Seas, my walk with Him can only deepen.

At times though, when God doesn't meet my expectations, I become offended. A wall is erected in my heart, and I begin to distance myself from Him. It's in those moments I need to repent and turn back to God to restore our relationship. One personal example of this was when we needed to cut John's salary and we had to do some jobs around the house ourselves instead of paying someone to do them. I then realized my disappointment sprang from the fact that I had presumed God would make things easier the older we got. The Holy Spirit showed me the ugliness of my presumption and pride. In humility, I confessed my sin to the Lord and received His forgiveness.

But perhaps the ultimate example of this is the biblical account of John the Baptist. Being in prison was likely not on John's list of expectations for being Jesus's forerunner. Especially when it looked as if he might die there, John had ample opportunity to become offended. But Jesus spoke with John's disciples and told them to tell John, "And blessed is the one who is not offended."[114]

What expectations have you had of God that were not met? Did you become offended?

Repenting of our offense at God for our hard times is a way we can pursue God by bridging the gap in our relationship. Conversely, using adversity and disillusionment to conform us to the image of His Son is one way that God pursues us. Thus, I have learned over the years that when I become disillusioned during a trial, instead of becoming offended, I can ask God what His redemptive purpose is in the adversity. For instance, one time I asked God why He was allowing me to suffer through a rough patch with a loved one. He told me that He was allowing it to make me look more like Him in the area of kindness. That one piece of insight gave me the grace I needed to be kind to the person who had hurt me. I wanted to develop God's character trait of kindness and not waste the trial.

Whether through adversity or triumph, however, the important thing is to take the time to pursue God. Communicate with Him by praying and listening to Him speak. Commit to a lifelong relationship with Him at the center. Ask God for His redemptive purpose during adversity. And keep the cycle of wholehearted devotion on constant repeat in your life — knowing, trusting, loving, and obeying God. Because He's always there, just waiting to be caught.

. . . . . . . . . . . . . . . . . . . . . . . .

## What I Heard My Father Say

*Run after me, my child; I will let you catch me. Pursue knowing me. Experience me through your daily life. Spend time with me reading the Word and listening to my voice to understand who I am and what attributes I possess. The goal is for you to love and trust me, which comes as you discover the truth about who I am as the Father, Son, and Holy Spirit. Remember, the greater you trust me, the greater your intimacy with me will be.*

**Take time to wait before the Lord.**
**Ask Him what He wants to say to you regarding this chapter.**

## ~ The Heart of the Matter ~

- The cycle of wholehearted devotion toward God is knowing, trusting, loving, and obeying God.
- Our enemy will do anything and everything to prevent us from accurately knowing God.
- Accurate and intimate knowledge of God results in accurate and intimate knowledge of who we are and who God created us to be.
- It's not enough to know *about* God; we must *experience* Him.
- We get to know God through communication and time spent together.
- There's a correlation between trust and intimacy. The greater our trust in God, the greater our intimacy with God.
- Trust is the foundation upon which all relationships are built.
- Relationships require commitment, and ours with God is no different.
- God is not one segment of my life; He is my life!
- Our perception of God — right or wrong — determines our destiny.
- Our circumstances or outcomes don't determine the truth of who God is.
- God is good even when the outcome or circumstances look bad.
- Sometimes, it's the not-so-good situations that best display the goodness of God. His goodness shines brightest in the dark.
- "God is good" is the "top button" that must align for everything else in life to align.
- The lens we see God through shapes how we relate to Him and how we reflect God to those we meet.
- When we know God better, we make Him better known.

— 7 —

# LOVING AND OBEYING GOD

*Jesus replied, "Anyone who loves me will obey my*
*teaching. My Father will love them, and we will*
*come to them and make our home with them."*

JOHN 14:23

Raphael Simon writes, "To fall in love with God is the greatest of all romances; to seek him, the greatest adventure; to find him, the greatest human achievement." When we know God, we can't help but trust and love God. And when we love God, obedience is close to follow, because we want to please the One we love. Mike Bickle says, "Obedience isn't earning God's love, it's the way we express our love to God."

My love stories with my husband, John, and the Lover of my soul, Jesus, share similarities.

Initially, I couldn't stop talking about John. He consumed my daily thoughts, and I only wanted to be with him. Being with him compelled me to think about the next time we could be together. It didn't matter where we were or why we were together, as long as we were together.

As I discovered John's likes and dislikes, I stored them away in my brain, waiting for a time I could use that knowledge to value him. I wanted to do things for him, and I desired to please him. After we were married, I'd cook his favorite meals, bring him coffee in bed as he woke up, and run errands for him, not out of duty but because I loved him. Likewise, John displayed his love toward me by listening to my heart, being affectionate, telling me he loved me (more!), taking me out on dates, and sharing his heart with me.

My love relationship with Jesus began similarly. When I was a new believer in high school, friends called me "Jesus Freak" because I talked about God constantly and my life revolved around activities of a Christian ministry called Young Life. I desired to please my "husband" Jesus because I loved Him, so I obeyed Him and did what He asked me to do. I spent time getting to know God through reading His Word and talking to Him through prayer. Jesus had my attention and affection.

Likewise, Jesus displayed His love for me by sharing secrets with me (more about this in the final chapter of this book), hearing my prayers, and answering them. I knew He cared and was involved in my life.

 Describe your love relationship with Jesus.

## Obstacles to Love

*Teach me your way, Lord, that I may rely*
*on your faithfulness; give me an undivided*
*heart, that I may fear your name.*

PSALM 86:11

My love relationship with the Lord started off right; I was head-over-heels, madly in love with Him. But slowly and subtly, my feelings of delight changed to feelings of duty. No longer did I simply want to please Him through my obedience; rather, I became more like a religious Pharisee, doing things to earn His love, which I had forgotten I already possessed.

The beauty of God's love for us is there is nothing we could ever do to earn it; and since that's the case, there's also nothing we could ever do to lose God's love for us. This truth creates a no-fear love relationship, where there is greater freedom to love. It's like the quote in the movie *Beyond the Mask*: "Neither redemption nor love can ever be earned." But after being a Christian for some time, my heart seemed to forget about this truth and my understanding of God's grace seemed to slip away. And as a result, my "first love" feelings for Him began to diminish.

Revelation 2:4–5a convicted me: "Yet I hold this against you: You have forsaken the love you had at first. Consider how far you have fallen! Repent and do the things you did at first." After thinking on this passage, I came to see that just as marriages can become stale, our love relationship with God can lose its passion and become stagnant. But I also realized there are three actions we can take when this happens in our love relationship with Jesus (and also, conveniently, in our marriage with our spouse!):

1. **Remember.** Recall what your love relationship was like in the beginning and reflect on "how far you've fallen" from that spot. This will initiate the road back to intimacy. Take time to consider God's attributes, who He's been to you, and how you've experienced Him in your life.

2. **Repent.** Identify and turn away from any sins, distractions, and other lovers or idols in your life and return to God. Allow genuine godly sorrow to lead you to confess your unrighteousness, seek God's forgiveness, and desire your relationship with Jesus to be restored.[115]

3. **Redo.** Do the things you did when you first fell in love with Jesus. Focus your heart on reacquainting yourself with who God is and on what He has done and will do. And as you spend time in His presence, your love for Jesus will be reignited.

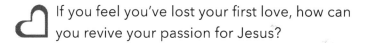 If you feel you've lost your first love, how can you revive your passion for Jesus?

Taking steps to refresh a stale love relationship is important; however, equally or more important is to be aware of obstacles that can keep us from being intimate with God in the first place. Once we learn to identify the obstacles, we can take measures to try to prevent or remove them. There can be any number of obstacles to closeness with God, but in my experience, two of the biggest ones are a divided heart and inattention.

## Obstacle 1: A Divided Heart

Our priorities reflect what we value, which is why God desires that we make Him our first priority in life. He wants us to value Him more than anyone or anything else and to have wholehearted devotion toward Him, being undivided in purpose, enthusiasm, and will. Charles Spurgeon wrote,

"A jealous God will not be content with a divided heart. He must be loved first and best."

In other words, God's most treasured possessions are the undivided hearts of His beloved children. God asks for this not because He is a power-hungry dictator or even because He needs our devotion. Rather, it's because He loves us and knows that He alone is able to give the long-lasting comfort we need and desire. He knows that any other god we worship won't fully satisfy, so He asks us to love Him wholeheartedly — with our whole being.

What does it mean to love Him with our whole being? Jesus answered this when He responded to the question "What is the greatest commandment?" in Matthew 22:36–38: "Love the Lord your God with all your heart and with all your soul and with all your mind." This same answer from Jesus is recorded in Mark 12:30 but adds "with all your strength." In other words, we're to love God with our entire physical, mental, emotional, and volitional being.

Loving God with our whole being can be compared to having eyes like a dove. Doves have monocular vision — they can focus on only one thing at a time. For this reason, these "love birds" are usually always watching their mates. I've observed doves out on our back deck. When one flies back onto the branch of a tree, the mate soon follows.

Song of Songs 1:15 describes believers this way: "How beautiful you are, my darling! Oh, how beautiful! Your eyes are doves." In this verse, God is implying that we should have eyes for only Him. And that we shouldn't become distracted and look at something or someone else.

### Idols

Another way to understand loving God with our whole being is to compare our relationship with Him to a marriage, in which our bridegroom Jesus desires an undivided heart from His bride. Consider what outside lovers do to a marriage relationship, even if the other "lovers" are not people but hobbies, work, ministry, or addictions. Anything that takes focus, time, and affection away from the spouse as the priority does not sit well with the relationship. The same goes for any other "lover" that takes focus, time, and affection away from God as our priority, which is why we are instructed not to have idols.

If you recall, an idol is anything or anyone we set up in place of or hold in higher esteem than God; we trust it to give us comfort and security and we give control to it in our lives. An idol is also a priority in our life. Our identity, worth, and significance are so tied to it that we feel if we lost it, life would no longer be worth living.

Having an idol, or worshiping or loving someone or something more than God, is idolatry. God is very clear on how He feels about idolatry: "You shall have no other gods before me."[116] The very first commandment, God's top mandate, is for us to love Him more than anyone or anything else. We also see in Deuteronomy 32:16 that our foreign gods and idols make God jealous, angering Him to the point of rejection.[117] Idolatry can even bring God's judgment upon us[118] with the consequence of God humbling us.[119]

God's great love for us causes Him to be jealous when rivals, or false lovers, compete for our love for Him. God will not stand for *any* lover to come between us and Him!

### Why We Turn to Idols

The Israelites, in Exodus 32:1, became impatient and afraid as they waited for Moses to come down from the mountain, so they asked Aaron to make them "gods who will go before us." We, too, often turn to idols because we are insecure, anxious, dissatisfied, discontent, or uncomfortable. Idols can also form as a result of hurt, offense, or emotional wounds that haven't been healed. We might become impatient and fearful while waiting for the Lord to answer our prayers. Or we may become discontent if they're not answered as we desire. Whatever the discomfort, our response is often to take matters into our own hands. We try to control the situation or comfort ourselves by turning to an idol. But the more satisfaction we find in God, the less we will try to find it in idols.

> Describe a time when you grew impatient, like the Israelites, and took matters into your own hands instead of trusting God.

In my own life, because my dad was not emotionally present for me in my growing-up years, getting approval and acceptance from men became an idol. Once my hurt was healed through acceptance in Jesus, however, I became free and no longer needed what my dad was unable to give me. Another go-to god I held in the past, especially when I was anxious, was food. I immediately ran to the pantry or refrigerator for comfort, trusting and believing that food would give me the security I needed, more than God could. Other times, I escaped the stress of life by immersing myself in a novel or talking to friends. On one occasion, I tried calling three different girlfriends to share my latest struggle with them and to ask them for prayer. When not one of them answered the phone, I heard the Lord whisper, *"What about me? Talk to me about your struggles before you reach out to a friend for help. I want to be the one who comforts and encourages you."*

Eventually, I learned to run to God, my true passion, first, knowing I could find my comfort and security in Him. This became clear to me when we moved from Omaha to Wichita. Before the move, I had feared I would feel lonely and abandoned in our new city. But after our move, I was surprised to find that, even though I initially had only a few friends and spent a good deal of time alone, I did not feel lonely. I knew God was with me. And my relationship with Him had deepened to the point that He was enough. It was then that I realized how tempting it is to think that our idols will rid us of loneliness, when in actuality, we perpetuate our loneliness by choosing other gods to meet our need for intimacy. In reality, our loneliness disappears only when we're truly intimate with the Lord.

Identify the idols in your life and describe the reasons you place your trust in them.

*Why Idols Are a Problem*

Although the apostle John admonishes us to "keep yourselves from idols," we still fall for them because we think they will somehow comfort and rescue us.[120] In the end, however, they do more damage than good. Here are just a few of the negative repercussions of turning to idols:

- **Idols provide only *temporary* satisfaction.**[121] For some reason we think our idols of food, shopping, exercise, television, movies, Facebook, sleep, alcohol, sex, pornography, or possessions will somehow meet our needs and satisfy the longings of our hearts. But that never happens, at least not for the long term.

- **Idols cause us to turn away from God and His commands**. We end up worshiping our idols, putting our trust in them[122] instead of placing our firm belief in the Trustworthy One. As a result, they can cause us to forget God[123] and become unfaithful to Him.[124]

- **Idols control our lives, taking our time, health, focus, and money.** Idols take away from us and don't give back. We can end up sacrificing so much of ourselves and our time, attention, affection, and money on idols, because they always leave us wanting for more. And over time, we can become like marionette puppets, our idols attached so tightly to our heartstrings that they jerk us this way and that, controlling our lives. In contrast, when we sacrifice for God, He gives back to us, and we find true, lasting satisfaction in Him.

- **Idolatry brings shame and disgrace upon us.**[125] One of the saddest truths is found in Jeremiah 2:11b: "But my people have exchanged their glorious God for worthless idols." Similarly, Romans 1:25 (TPT) says, "They traded the truth of God for a lie. They worshiped and served the things God made rather than the God who made all things." We can't have idols and expect God's glory too! Isaiah 46:9 sums it up well: "Remember the former things, those of long ago; I am God, and there is no other; I am God, and there is none like me."

- **Idols are impotent, lacking in power and strength.** According to Scripture, idols can't see, hear, eat, or smell;[126] they can't save us from trouble and won't answer our prayers;[127] they're worthless and profit us nothing;[128] they don't do any good;[129] and they're powerless and ineffective.[130] In contrast, the Word says God is powerful and mighty;[131] He's true, alive, and eternal;[132] He keeps us safe;[133] and what He has said and planned will happen.[134] Idols are like broken cisterns[135] — they seep through, fail to provide what we need, and don't give what they promise. In contrast, when we worship God, He will always be faithful to fulfill our hearts. As Psalm 86:8 (TPT) says, "God, there's no one like you; there's no other god as famous as you. You outshine all others and your miracles make it easy to know you."

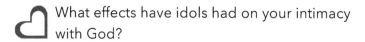 What effects have idols had on your intimacy with God?

*How to Tear Down Idols*

In the Bible, we're encouraged to flee, or run away from, idolatry.[136] But what if we find that, like the Israelites, we have already run toward an idol and clung to it? Just as the Israelites were instructed to tear down the Asherah poles,[137] we are admonished to put our idols to death.

To do this, first recognize your idols and admit their inability to satisfy. Ask yourself the reason you need comfort from the idol. Then identify the lie at the root of that reasoning and replace it with God's truth.

Once you recognize your idols, renounce them; that is, refuse to follow them and then repent, or turn around, and walk away.

Finally, take steps to replace your idols with greater intimacy with God. In the same way that we are to "leave [our families] and cleave [to our spouses]" in order to have a healthy earthly marriage, we must also leave our idols and cleave to our heavenly Bridegroom to have a solid relationship with Him. To do this, ask God for His help in breaking the hold the false god has over your heart. Then return to the Lord and worship only Him. Real freedom comes when God alone is your source of comfort.

> What steps will you take to demolish the idols in your life so that you have an undivided heart for God?

## Obstacle 2: Inattention

Passion is like a fire. Fires in the natural world automatically die down unless you tend to them and continually fuel the flames. It is the same with your relationship fire. You must tend and pay regular attention to it so that, should it start to die down, you can "use a poker" to move the logs a bit so they get more oxygen and keep burning. There are several ways to do this.

One simple way I stoke the fire of my love for the Lord is by periodically **asking the Holy Spirit to cause me to fall more madly in love with Him.** God initiates each aspect of our relationship with Him, so He enjoys it when we ask to be hungrier for Him and the things of God.

Second, just as best friends or spouses **spend time together**, face to face, to enhance their relationship, we must spend time with God, seeking to hear and understand His word, both in the *logos* sense and the *rhema* sense. The Greek terms *logos* and *rhema* both translate to "God's word" in English, but in its original language, *logos* refers to the written word of God (or Scripture), while *rhema* refers to God's "spoken" word to me, which might illuminate how I apply a particular scripture to my life or how I handle an aspect of my walk with God. Christianity.com describes *rhema* as seeing "how Scripture's universal truths apply to your life personally," and *Charisma* magazine gives this example: "The rhema word can happen when you're reading a particular passage of Scripture, perhaps one you have seen many times before, and you see it in a new light and see how it applies to your life personally."

To fuel the flame in your relationship with God, spend time in the *logos* word by reading the Song of Solomon, which describes how your heavenly Bridegroom feels about you. Read and understand passages such as Psalm 45:11a, which says, "Let the king be enthralled by your beauty." And let Scripture woo you back into your bridegroom's embrace. Spend time in the *rhema* word by sharing your heart with God through prayer, sitting still to listen to His voice, and hearing Him share His heart with you. Record these *rhema* words that God speaks to you in a journal, and then obey whatever He says.

Another way to turn up the fire for Jesus in your heart is to **spend time with those who are passionate about God.** Passion is contagious! For instance, I once had a godly mentor, in her late nineties, who, after many years, still kissed the glass that covered a print she had of Jesus's face. Her love for Jesus was obvious as she recounted personal stories highlighting God's faithfulness and power in her life. And every time I listened to her testify of Jesus's love and goodness toward her, it drew me closer to Him. **Reading or listening to other peoples' testimonies** in this way blows upon the embers of our love for God, encouraging our hearts and building our faith as a result.

On the flip side, when I **share testimonies of God's goodness with others**, it also fuels the flame, reminding me how much God loves me. I remember His kindness, goodness, and faithfulness toward me, and it causes me to scoot a little closer to Him. That's why, at my sixtieth birthday party, after we enjoyed a yummy brunch, I took time to testify about milestones in my life when I had seen God come through for me. With each milestone I spoke about, I placed a physical stone in front of me, building a memorial of God's faithfulness, stone after stone, just like the Israelites did. But I was encouraged as I realized that it was difficult to limit my testimonies to just a handful of physical stones, since, as Psalm 40:5 says, "Many, Lord my God, are the wonders you have done … were I to speak and tell of your deeds, they would be too many to declare."

**Having an attitude of gratitude toward God** also helps maintain our passion. Thanking God for who He is and honoring Him with our thanksgiving gives Him great pleasure. When we humble ourselves and give tribute to God with our gratefulness, His presence and glory become evident.[138]

> Make a list of ways God has been kind toward you. Spend time thanking Him.

In addition, in the same way some earthly couples renew their marriage vows, we can **recommit our hearts to him in oneness and faithfulness**, taking time to tell the Lord how much we love Him. At times I've done this, repeating out loud to Jesus, "I need you, I want you, I have to have you."

**Fasting** also tenderizes our hearts and draws us closer into God's presence, as we have to depend upon Him to supply us with His physical strength. And finally, **obedience** establishes greater oneness with the Lover of our souls.

> Name one specific way you will intentionally stoke the fire of your love for God.

## Love Obeys

*If you love me, keep my commands. Whoever has my commands and keeps them is the one who loves me.*

JOHN 14:15, 21

You might ask, "What does obeying God have to do with loving God?" Everything! Jesus made it crystal clear in the verse above: our love for and obedience to God are directly linked.

In fact, Jesus was the epitome of this link, showing His love both for His Father and for us by being obedient even unto death on a cross.[139] Note, however, that when God the Father first spoke of His love and approval for His Son, Jesus, it was before Jesus had even begun His ministry: "When all the people were being baptized, Jesus was baptized too. And as he was praying, heaven was opened and the Holy Spirit descended on him in bodily form like a dove. And a voice came from heaven: 'You are my Son, whom I love; with you I am well pleased.'"[140]

If you're a parent, you have probably experienced this kind of love firsthand. Think about it: when did you first feel love for your son or daughter? Was it after they were old enough to obey you? Or was it when, as newborns, they cried, slept, ate, and pooped? If you're like me, you fell in love with them even before that, while they were in the womb. You loved them not because they obeyed you or because of anything they did; rather, you loved them because they were yours.

In the same way, God the Father wasn't saying He loved or was pleased with Jesus because of Jesus's obedience or any other thing that Jesus *did*; rather, He felt love and pleasure for Jesus simply because Jesus was His Son. So Jesus didn't need to obey God in order to earn His heavenly Father's love. Rather, He already had God's love. And, in turn, He loved God, which motivated Him to obey.

It is the same with us. God loves us not because we obey Him, but because we are His! We don't need to obey Him in order to earn His love; we already have it. Rather, we obey God because we know we are loved by God. We know that He is good and loving and all-knowing, so we trust that He has our best interest in mind and can see a bigger picture than we can. But we also obey God because *we* love *Him*. When we love someone, we want to please them.

## Other Motivators of Obedience

Of course, it is still possible to obey someone you don't love, whether it be out of obligation or fear or pride. I have seen in my life, love-driven obedience lasts longer and is better in the long run than obedience driven by any other factor. Obedience not motivated by a love relationship can lead to legalism, bitterness, or burnout.

Consider the kind of obedience the Pharisees displayed. They obeyed out of duty and followed a list of rules they could check off. It had nothing to do with wanting to please the God they loved; rather, the Pharisees' religious spirit had to do with wanting to look good to man. It was an issue of pride. But if you are motivated by the approval of man, which is often temporary, you will give up caring about obedience as soon as you no longer have that approval.

If you are motivated to obey God out of fear or obligation, that is also destined to fail in the long run. Being afraid of God and the harsh consequences that might follow disobedience may control your behavior, but it will not help your heart. You may become bitter against God, blaming Him for your spirit of fear. Or you may give up trying to obey whenever you fail or don't get what you expect from Him, feeling it's not worth your time and effort.

In all of these cases, the will to obey is not backed up by a healthy relationship with God, so it will eventually die out. As with an earthly marriage, the key to sticking it out through "better or worse" is a solid love relationship. If your loyalty were based only on the gifts you received from your spouse, you would be less motivated to stay in the marriage the moment you received something you didn't want or expect. Likewise, if your willingness to obey and stick with Jesus is based only on what you receive from Him, that willingness will inevitably diminish the moment He doesn't give you what you expect. But if you obey out of your love for Him, you will remain faithful to your heavenly Bridegroom, even when adversity hits.

Finally, if you are motivated to obey because you think it will earn you more love from God, remember that this is impossible. God doesn't love us more when we obey Him or love us less when we sin. Whether we're prideful or humble, self-centered or selfless, obedient or disobedient, God can't help but love us — but only because He is love and we are His children. God's love for us is based on who He is and on what Jesus did for us on the cross, not on how well we obey Him. One way to think about this is to remember a time when you obeyed God and another time when you were disobedient and rebellious. Do you know that God's love for you was the same in both instances? If you're a parent, you can probably more closely identify with this kind of love; it's the same kind of love we have for our own children.

Sometimes my children do things I may not agree with, but that doesn't change my love for them one bit. God feels the same way about us. There's nothing we could ever do or say to make God love us more or less than He already does.

 What is your motivation to obey God?

## What Obedience Looks Like

*As obedient children, do not conform to the evil*
*desires you had when you lived in ignorance. But just*
*as he who called you is holy, so be holy in all you do.*

I PETER 1:14–15

Healthy obedience to God is rooted in love. But what does that kind of healthy obedience look like in real life? What does it require of us? What kinds of challenges and blessings does it bring? Here are a few characteristics to keep in mind as we navigate through a life of obedience:

### Obedience Is an Act of Worship

The first mention of the word *worship* in the Bible took place after God asked Abraham to "take your son, your only son, whom you love — Isaac — and go to the region of Moriah. Sacrifice him there as a burnt offering on a mountain I will show you."[141] A few verses later, Abraham equates his act of obedience with worship. And toward the end of that chapter, God tells Abraham that all of the nations on earth would be blessed "because you have obeyed me."

In the New Testament, Romans 12:1 reinforces this idea of sacrificial obedience as worship: "Therefore, I urge you, brothers and sisters, in view of God's mercy, to offer your bodies as a living sacrifice, holy and pleasing to God — this is your true and proper worship."

## Obedience May Be Sacrificial

On September 16, 2012, Pastor Craig Groeschel of Life Church tweeted, "Sacrifice is giving up something you love for something you love more." Often, obedience requires that we die to ourselves and "take up our cross," as Jesus did in the Garden of Gethsemane, saying, "Not my will, but Thy will be done."[142] In other words, obedience requires us to surrender our own will to God's. We become a living sacrifice, submitting our words, thoughts, actions, will, and emotions to the Lordship of Jesus Christ.

I experienced this kind of sacrificial obedience when I answered God's call to go on a mission trip to Kabul, Afghanistan, while the Taliban was trying to take control of the city by bombing it. I heard the bombs go off, observed families standing in line to get bowls of rice, witnessed a bombed-out operating room full of maimed children, and — once I returned home — paid the price with Post-Traumatic Stress Disorder (PTSD). I emotionally shut down, unable to feel happy or sad or anything in between, unless triggered by certain situations. It was only after time, through a process of praying and sharing what I had seen, heard, and felt with a few close friends, that I was able to surrender my emotions back to Jesus's control, letting Him protect me.

Whenever we sacrifice in order to obey God, we can take comfort in knowing that God will help us and bless us through any difficulty we experience and use it for His good. We can also rest assured in knowing that Jesus doesn't ask anything of us that He wasn't also willing to give. After all, Christ demonstrated the ultimate sacrificial obedience on our behalf: "And being found in appearance as a man, he humbled himself and became obedient to death, even death on a cross."[143]

## Obedience Should Be Immediate and Complete

Many years ago, while reading Bible studies on parenting, I learned that "delayed obedience is disobedience." For example, if a parent asked their eight-year-old daughter to stop playing with her toys to go clean up her room but she continued to play anyway, her delay in obeying would actually be considered disobedience. In the same vein, if you know God is asking you to do something, it is best to act on it at once: "If anyone, then, know the good they ought to do and doesn't do it, it is sin for them."[144]

Partial obedience is also the same as disobedience. This principle is clearly displayed in 1 Samuel 15, when the prophet Samuel instructs King Saul to attack and totally destroy the Amalekites. Saul follows through but does only part of the job, keeping Agag, the king, alive and sparing the best sheep and cattle. Saul later confesses that he didn't fully obey the Lord because he feared men, and his disobedience reaps rejection from God.[145]

## Obedience to God in the Little Things Will Help Us with Obedience to Him in the Big Things

Each time we're obedient to God, it makes it easier to obey Him the next time. When John and I first married, we met with a Christian friend who was an insurance agent. He emphasized the importance of God's command to us to tithe — or to give back to God a tenth of our gross salary. We embraced the principle, even in those first years of marriage when we had little money. It was challenging at times, but it drilled into us the practice of tithing. Later, when John became a physician and his salary increased, we didn't hesitate to continue tithing, even though it meant giving more, because our hearts and minds had already been trained to obey.

## Obstacles to Obedience

*Does the Lord delight in burnt offerings
and sacrifices as much as in obeying the
Lord? To obey is better than sacrifice, and
to heed is better than the fat of rams.*

1 SAMUEL 15:22

The enemy does not want us to obey the Lord. In fact, he will set roadblocks in our path to prevent us from obeying God. A major roadblock that causes me to struggle with obeying is fear that God will ask me to do something risky and out of my comfort zone. This is not an unrealistic expectation; He does do this, and He has done this with me. But whenever I have chosen to obey, He has also faithfully equipped me with whatever I needed to follow through. And in the aftermath of my obedience, I always realize that He is worth any amount of discomfort I had to go through to obey Him. Take, for instance, the time I rode in an armed vehicle from Peshawar, Pakistan, toward Kabul, Afghanistan, and we stopped at a "rest stop" to use the facilities: two holes in the ground on top of a small hill. Surrounding the holes was a wall, shaped in a half circle, that was only about three feet high. When I rounded the wall, I realized that, unfortunately, many people before us had missed the holes. The situation was disconcerting and a little embarrassing, but after relieving myself, I climbed down the small hill and said, "Only for Jesus!" God is worthy of our obedience as a display of our love for Him.

Another obstacle to obedience is loving ourself more than we love God. We may love God, but if we don't love Him more than we love ourself, it will be harder to obey Him, especially in the long term. Loving God more than we love ourself, however, will help us to obey Him until the day we die. And the more we love Him, the more we will obey Him. Even when it might cost us something. That's why the apostle Paul encourages us in 2 Corinthians 5:9 to shift from being a self-worshiper to a worshiper of God, so that "we make it our goal to please him."

Additional obstacles to obedience can include fear of man (I want others' approval, so I avoid holding them accountable in love, even though God requests it); love of comfort and pleasure (I avoid fasting despite the Word's instruction to, or I read my novel instead of obeying God to write); lack of trust in God (I take control over a situation instead of submitting to His will); idolatry (I revolve my life around satisfying the demands of my idol rather than satisfying my heavenly Father, who loves and wants the best for me); and rebellion (I refuse to say no to myself and yes to God, adopting an attitude that our pastor's wife defines as, "I want to do what I want to do, when I want to do it").

What obstacle to obedience do you struggle with the most?

# The Blessings of Obedience

*Hear, Israel, and be careful to obey so that it may
go well with you and that you may increase greatly
in a land flowing with milk and honey, just as the
Lord, the God of your ancestors, promised you.*

DEUTERONOMY 6:3

As a young mom many years ago, I heard Elisabeth Elliot speak at a women's retreat in Sedona, Arizona, and she said something that has stayed with me: "Obedience brings blessing."[146] Our acts of obedience will not only lead to blessing but also cause a ripple effect of blessing. So we never know where one act of obedience might lead. Think about Luke 5:2–11, when Jesus instructs the fishermen where to put their nets; their obedience to Him not only gains them lots of fish but leads them to become "fishers of men" for generations to come!

How have you experienced God's blessing as a result of your obedience? Describe a time when one act of obedience had a ripple effect.

Whatever the cost of our obedience, the resulting blessing will be worth it. After all, the reason God calls for obedience is because of its benefit: "What does the Lord your God ask of you but to fear the Lord your God, *to walk in obedience to Him*, to love Him, to serve the Lord your God with all your heart and with all your soul, and to observe the Lord's commands and decrees that I am giving you today *for your own good*."[147] Scripture shows us a number of benefits that can occur as the result of our obedience to God:

- It builds deeper intimacy with God. Jesus, in John 14:23, says, "Anyone who loves me will obey my teaching. My Father will love them, and we will come to them and make our home with them." The result of our obedience, then, is that the Father, Son, and Holy Spirit will come to us and make their abode with us. Because of this, we can think of each act of obedience as a step closer toward God.

- God covers and protects us, releasing His supernatural power, glory, and favor upon us.[148]
- We are found trustworthy by God, resulting in His giving us greater entrustments.[149]
- His destiny is fulfilled in our lives, and our dreams become reality.[150]
- We receive the fruits of peace, rest, and contentment, and we become more Christlike and spiritually mature.[151]
- God gives us adventure.[152]
- Others are affected for the good.[153]

Just as obedience brings blessings, in the same manner, our disobedience aborts those blessings.[154] In other words, just as there are benefits to obeying, there are also natural consequences to disobeying. Feeling distant from God and lacking in His presence tops the list of consequences, since, just as each act of obedience is a step closer to God, each act of disobedience is a step away. Disobeying can also mean seeing our dreams and destinies delayed or denied, as it did for the Israelites, whose frequent disobedience kept them wandering forty years before they found the Promised Land. As seen in Jonah 1:4–5, our disobedience can also have a ripple effect, as others can suffer from our rebellion. And finally, we can bring defeat and destruction upon ourselves when we disobey. Remember Jonah? Initially, when God requested him to go to Nineveh to preach against their wickedness, Jonah ran away. The result: he landed in the belly of a huge fish until he repented three days later.[155]

Potential blessings and consequences should not be what drive us to obey God, however, because the highest form of obedience is not motivated by reward but by a sincere love for God. It is with this heart attitude that we must follow the instruction that Jesus's mother gave the servants at the wedding in Cana: "Do whatever he tells you."[156] We will always be glad we did.

. . . . . . . . . . . . . . . . . . . . . . . .

## What I Heard My Father Say

*Oh, how I love you! I am grateful you are my beloved child. Show me your love for me through your wholehearted devotion and obedience. When your passion for me begins to wane, stoke the fire of your love. Don't let other lovers, such as idols, get in the way of our relationship. I want to be the one you run to for comfort and security. I'm jealous to be your "one and only."*

**Take time to wait before the Lord.**
**Ask Him what He wants to say to you regarding this chapter.**

# ~ The Heart of the Matter ~

- When there is no fear in a love relationship, there is greater freedom to love.
- Idols provide temporary satisfaction, control our lives, lack power and strength, and cause us to forget or turn away from God.
- We have to recognize our idols and admit their inability to satisfy before we're able to overcome them.
- We need to stoke the fire of our love for the Lord.
- The secret to sinning less is to love God more.
- Our love for God and our obedience to God go hand in hand.
- Obedience is the way we show or prove our love to God, but it's our love for God that motivates us to obey.
- Obedience not motivated by a love relationship leads to legalism.
- Relationship-driven obedience is better in the long run than fear-driven obedience.
- We obey what or whom we love.
- Our obedience is the way we worship God. It's to be immediate and complete, and it is sometimes sacrificial.
- Obedience is for our benefit. It builds our intimacy with God, brings us blessing, and fulfills God's destiny for our lives.
- Each act of obedience moves us closer to God.
- We never know where one act of obedience will take us or when it will have an effect on others.

# — 8 —
# SEALING YOUR IDENTITY IN CHRIST

*Therefore, if anyone is in Christ, the new creation
has come: The old has gone, the new is here!*

2 CORINTHIANS 5:17

Getting to know God not only helps us to love and obey Him, but it also gives us a better understanding of who we are — of our identity as His son or daughter. The more we know God, the more accurately we will be able to see ourselves through God's eyes and the more liberated we will become to be who He has created us to be. And when that happens, God shines through us and receives the glory.

In the Bible, a person's identity was often defined by a prophetic declaration of his or her name at birth. At times, though, God would alter someone's birth name to signify a change in that person's character or anointing. When the scope of Abram's ministry expanded, God gave him the new name Abraham, changing the meaning from "exalted father" to "father of a multitude." Jacob, meaning "the supplanter," became Israel, "one who prevailed with God." The apostle Paul started as Saul, and Jesus's disciple Simon was renamed Peter. Whenever God gave His people new names, it meant they were being transformed by Him, as if they were receiving a new identity. The names God gave His children were important.

To my husband and I, the names we gave our children were important too. With each pregnancy, we labored over the baby name book, trying to figure out what to call each child. We even considered possible nicknames for the monikers we liked, because we knew names have a way of marking people and shaping their identity.

I've never been fond of my first name, but this became especially true when the pastor, during our wedding ceremony, told me, "Norma, your name means 'lady of perfection.'" I rolled my eyes and sarcastically *thought, Oh, great!* I cringed, overwhelmed at the thought that I needed to be perfect to fulfill my namesake. But I later discovered a more favorable definition of Norma: "example of godliness."

Then in 1988, while driving, I heard God's voice in my mind, giving me a new name: Mary. I immediately thought of the story in Luke 10:38–42, when sisters Mary and Martha are visited by Jesus. This thought was surprising, however, because among the two women, I felt that I usually more closely resembled Martha. Martha, being "Miss hospitality," busies herself by preparing her house and a meal for Jesus. But while Martha is consumed with tasks, Mary is consumed with Jesus; she sits at His feet, hanging onto His every word. Martha becomes upset and demands that Jesus tell Mary to help her. But much to Martha's surprise, Jesus honors Mary, saying Mary has made the best choice. Years later, I would live up to the name of this Mary, who was consumed with her Lord, but at this time in my life, the name did not seem to fit.

The next time God gave me a life-altering name was in 1996 at a church leadership retreat. As the counseling pastor and his wife washed my feet, they prophesied the title "Daddy's Girl," over me, speaking to the great desire I'd had since I was a little girl: to feel special to my dad. Even though I may not have had my earthly dad's acceptance and attention, when I received this name, I knew that I held that special position with my heavenly Father.

Then as I prepared to run my first marathon in 1998, my girlfriend spoke the name "Bride" over me. She even bought me a bouquet of red roses to signify my engagement to the Lord. Until that time, I had felt more like a servant or a slave in my relationship with God, but now I held an intimate position — that of a bride.

And it was through the Muslim tour guide in a citadel in Syria whom God bestowed the name "Queen" upon me. After that moment, I no longer walked with my eyes down, burdened by the cloak of shame; I could now walk with my head held high, knowing I had God-given authority as royalty.

God saw me as each of these descriptive names before I resembled what they represented. It's the same thing He did when Gideon was threshing wheat hidden in a winepress, afraid of the Midianites. God called Gideon "mighty warrior." God gave Gideon this name because He knew who Gideon would become. In the same way, He knew I would eventually become a Mary who loved to be in His presence. The Lord is "the God who gives life to the dead and calls into being things that were not."[157] In other words, He gave me those new names as a way to help me see myself as He saw me. He wanted me to know myself through His eyes. And through the gift of new names, He assisted me to see and believe the truth about myself. God wanted to override the false self that reigned in my heart and mind so that my true self (who He created me to be) could be released. He desired to show me my true identity and who I would become, if only I believed Him. These new names birthed faith within me. I believed I would grow into them and eventually become who God says I am.

Has God given you any new names? If so, how have they spoken into being who you were to become?

Of course, there are other ways God can reveal our identity to us; He doesn't always do this by giving us a new name. But regardless of His method, until we see ourselves as God sees us, we won't be able to be who He's created us to be. Consider Exodus 3, when God calls Moses to deliver the Israelites from the Egyptians. Moses doubts God's call on his life. He says to God, "Who am I, that I should go to Pharaoh and bring the Israelites out of Egypt?"[158] Moses feels insecure, unsure that he can do what God asked him to. Only through dialogue with God can Moses come to believe that God is with him and has called him to lead and deliver the Israelites from their slavery.

Like Moses, I have wrestled with God's call on my life. Before becoming a writer, for instance, I made a lengthy list with all the reasons I believed God had chosen the wrong woman to write for Him. God patiently waited for me to finish the list and said, *"That is exactly why I chose you! For when you are weak, I am free to be strong. When others see me come through for you, I will be the one to receive all the glory."* So after accepting this part of who God said I was, I then exercised my will in agreement with the Holy Spirit. God said I am a writer; therefore, I chose to agree with Him and obey Him by writing. I aligned my actions with my beliefs about my identity in Christ.

This is the way it is for all of us: we live out of our identities. And in this way, our destinies are formed.

> Sit still in the Lord's presence. Ask the Holy Spirit to show you who He sees you as.

# Identity Theft

*The thief comes only to steal and kill and destroy; I have come that they may have life, and have it to the full.*

JOHN 10:10

In the natural world, identity theft is on the rise. Identity theft is when someone illegally gains access to your personal information and uses it to open new accounts or make purchases. If you've ever noticed a charge in your bank account or on your credit card bill for something you didn't purchase, you've been a victim of identity theft. All too often, however, victims don't notice the violation until the damage has already been done.

In the spiritual world, another type of identity theft, instigated by Satan, also often occurs when we're unaware. A data breach happens: Satan takes our personal information without our knowledge and uses it against us. He attacks our character by telling us we're not good enough or that we're worthless, rejected, ugly, or stupid. He puts thoughts into our heads that make us believe we're not who God says we are and God isn't who He says He is. And before we realize it, we start to notice costly deficits in our "spiritual account" that we don't remember agreeing to. By then, the damage has been done: we have been hacked. We unwittingly bought into the lies, and now our identity has become so distorted that we appear more like orphans than the sons and daughters of God that we are. And when that happens, our destiny is thwarted. We feel condemned and hopeless, held captive by the enemy's words. Our identity has been stolen.

How has Satan stolen your true identity?

The speaker at a women's retreat I once attended handed out two blank name tags to each of the participants. On one of them, we were to write our name along with a phrase describing how we saw ourselves. I wrote, "Norma is not special." The speaker then directed us to sit quietly for a few minutes and ask God how He saw us. In those quiet moments, God whispered into my heart, *"You are made for greatness."* Two totally different statements about my identity, depending on the source — and my thoughts, feelings, and behavior would spring from the one I chose to believe.

What do your actions say you're believing – God's truth or Satan's lies?

We all have this choice: to believe the accuser of the brethren or the Lover of our souls. When I believe the lies of the enemy, Satan receives the credit; but when I have faith in what God the Father says about me, He receives the glory. Further, we will think, feel, act, and speak out based on who we choose to believe. For both these reasons, it's vital to believe what God says about us.

What does God say about you? Even if you feel you haven't heard Him tell you who you are personally, there is plenty of evidence in His Word about how He feels about each of His children — including you. Here are just a few of those viewpoints: God sees us as beautiful,[159] gifted,[160] chosen,[161] valuable,[162] and good enough.[163] Scripture also says God delights in us[164] and that we are unconditionally loved and accepted.[165] And God is for us, not against us.[166]

In contrast, the enemy will tell you the following lies (among others): that your past defines who you are and who you will become; that you will never be enough, especially in comparison to others; and that your significance and worth depend solely on your actions. In the following three sections, we'll combat those lies with God's truth.

## Truth: Your Past Does Not Define You

*Brothers and sisters, I do not consider myself yet to*
*have taken hold of it. But one thing I do: Forgetting*
*what is behind and straining toward what is ahead,*
*I press on toward the goal to win the prize for which*
*God has called me heavenward in Christ Jesus.*

PHILIPPIANS 3:13–14

"Our perpetual agreement with past experience creates the biggest strongholds that block the purposes of God in our lives," Steve Backlund writes. "This creation of our identities from our past causes us to think wrongly and be restricted in our life experience."

One big aspect of our past experiences that we often agree with, thus allowing it to shape our identity, is sin. If we haven't fully received God's forgiveness for the sins in our past, we won't be able to see ourselves as God sees us and, therefore, we will not be able to move forward in freedom. As Backland describes it, we will "be restricted in our life experiences," both present and future.

It's important to note, however, that there is a difference between intellectually acknowledging that we've been forgiven and truly believing and accepting that that's the case. It's easy to ask for forgiveness and then go on our merry way, knowing in our heads that we've done what we should do — but not really believing that we've been set free in our hearts. So even though we're forgiven, if our heart doesn't believe this truth, we won't act as if it's reality. In other words, we will continue to live as if we are in bondage to sin, and this belief — rather than the truth — will be what determines our identity. I know this from experience. More than once, I have continued to live under the shame of sins I committed, even after I asked for and received forgiveness for them, until the Holy Spirit gave me a heart revelation of His forgiveness.

When we're forgiven, our life's blackboard and all the sins written upon it, has been washed and completely cleansed. He's removed our sin "as far as the east is from the west."[167]

We've all sinned, which is why Jesus came to rescue us. But we have to remember that Jesus paid for our sins, once and for all. When we don't fully receive God's forgiveness, it's as if what Jesus did on the cross was not good enough. So after you've confessed and repented of your sin, stop allowing the enemy to attack you with his lies. Don't allow Satan to slander your character and whisper in your ear, "You're disqualified," because of a particular sin you've committed. Sometimes it's that very sin God uses and redeems to equip you for ministry. We are not who our past says we are; we are who the Word of God declares us to be.

> Is there any past sin for which you haven't fully received God's forgiveness within your head and heart? How have past sins or feeling disqualified prevented you from moving forward into God's destiny?

Finally, not only is our identity not based on the sins we've committed in the past; it is also not based on sins we will commit in the future. Our identity is based not in what we think, nor what others think; it's clarified and solidified through God's eyes and what He thinks about us.

## Truth: You Are Enough

*The tongue has the power of life and death.*

PROVERBS 18:21A

The enemy likes to make us believe that we will never be enough — whether that be good enough, smart enough, attractive enough, successful enough, and the list goes on. Feeling less-than can inhibit us from doing what God asks of us and knows we're capable of, making us ineffectual for the Lord. Two big ways the enemy does this is through self-criticism and self-comparison.

### Self-Criticism

Words are powerful. They have the power to speak life — or death — to our true identities in Christ. Words of criticism, in particular, speak death, crippling us from becoming who we really are as God's child. And words of self-criticism often start out as words spoken over us by others. Even years later, after we have forgiven our offenders, we can still remember and personalize their hurtful words.

I want to speak life, not death, over myself, so that I can live fully in my identity in Christ. I used to look down on myself because I thought I had a simple mindset and was a "low-capacity" person; for example, even though I love to ponder God's Word and understand His heart, I am not one to read nonfiction, which requires me to really think about what is being said. I'm also not good at juggling many things at once, and I am now learning that I have physical limits and need recovery after a busy season. I realized, though, that if I really believed "I am fearfully and wonderfully made; your works are wonderful,"[168] I wouldn't think or speak negatively about myself or others. I asked God to help me to stop selling myself short, before the words even left my mouth, and after time, I began to recognize His wisdom in making me the way I am. My "simplistic" mindset is actually a "big-picture" mindset that helps me to teach others in a way that they can grasp what I'm saying. Being a "low-capacity" person is a built-in safeguard to protect my heart that wants to minister all the time. Now, instead of complaining to God about my shortcomings, I am thankful for how He's made me and see the beauty in His design.

> How have you experienced the "power of life and death" in the words spoken over you?

I'm so grateful God doesn't let me get away with things that are not for my benefit. I'm thankful He calls me to account and convicts me of my sin of self-criticizing. It's His way to help me see myself as He sees me and to grow in self-acceptance and love. I've also been thankful for friends who have held me accountable, calling me out whenever I've spoken about my weaknesses in a way that I put myself down.

> In what ways has self-criticism kept you from becoming all who God created you to be?

## Self-Comparison

Comparing ourselves with others and feeling we come up short is another trap of the enemy we can fall into. Comparison is like bringing out a yardstick to measure who we are in contrast with others. It's a form of judgment we make upon ourselves, and Scripture points out its foolishness: "We do not dare to classify or compare ourselves with some who commend themselves. When they measure themselves by themselves and compare themselves with themselves, they are not wise."[169]

For me, this means being careful not to judge myself and my ministry based on my assessment of other people and their ministries. It's easy to compare myself as a speaker or writer with others and become discontent with who I am, wanting to become like them. When I find myself slipping into this mindset, I lean on 1 Corinthians 7:17, which says, "Nevertheless, each person should live as a believer in whatever situation the Lord has assigned to them, just as God has called them." In other words, God's not asking us to be like someone else; He's only asking us to be who He has created us to be.

Comparison kills who we really are and who God created us to be. We're not free to be fully alive in our God-given identity when we're focused on someone else's attributes and trying to be like them.

 How has the comparison trap kept you from living fully alive as God's child?

## Truth: You Are Significant

*When the woman saw that the fruit of the tree was good for food and pleasing to the eye, and also desirable for gaining wisdom, she took some and ate it.*

GENESIS 3:6A

Significance is "the quality of being important." God planted within each of us a desire for significance and self-worth, which we can find in and through Him. But the enemy twists God's truth about where our significance can be found.

Far too many years of my life were spent believing the lie that I could find significance in what I did. This lie grew from a false belief I had bought into, which said that if something is not productive, it's a waste of time. As a result, I believed that I was special whenever people needed me, and I thought my worth and value came through helping others. My significance came from *doing*, not *being*; therefore, I sought my value and identity through involvement in ministry.

The fallout from my faulty mentality was that I didn't know how to have fun, because I equated recreation with frivolity. I'd feel guilty participating in recreational activities before completing my responsibilities. I also didn't understand the importance of self-care. I continued giving more and more of myself out without ever pausing to replenish myself through rest and recreation. This eventually led to burnout. I was a car running on empty — and eventually I hit a wall and could go no further.

> Where do you find your value and significance?

## Slave or Son?

For many years of my ministry, I felt I had to earn my position as God's daughter, but it hadn't started out this way. When I initially became a Christian, God's grace had been new and fresh, I and fell in love with Him as my Father. Gradually, however, Satan's lies deceived me, and I forgot about living in grace, instead living by the law and by the work of my own hands. I became religious and following the rules, running myself ragged to try to earn my position as God's child. As a result, I adopted the identity of a slave rather than as God's daughter, and my relationship with Him became more duty than delight.

I mentioned previously that a major part of our identity is how we see ourselves in relation to our Father. One way to identify that relationship, then, is to ask yourself the question, "Do I feel more like God's slave or His son or daughter?" The way you answer can shed light on the thoughts, emotions, words, and behaviors that spring from that relationship and that ultimately form your identity. The following table shows some of the main differences between the two.

| Slaves | Sons |
|---|---|
| They are not heirs to their master's inheritance. | The inherit their father's estate. |
| They are paid to perform their duties. | They experience privileges because of their birth into the family. |
| Their role implies captivity. | Their role implies liberty. |
| Their obedience is motivated by fear. | Their obedience is motivated by love.[170] |
| They have a distant relationship with their master. | They can have an intimate relationship with their father. |
| Their master issues commands. | Their father offers communication. |

Notice that slaves and sons both submit to authority, but beyond that, their mentalities hold little similarity. The key difference between the two mentalities is the presence of shame. Shame promotes the slave mentality, and we perpetuate it by living under the law and trying to earn our salvation. On the other hand, by accepting grace, God's free gift to each of us through Jesus's sacrifice, we can rid ourselves of shame and wear the rightful mentality of God's child.

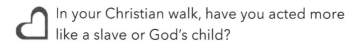 In your Christian walk, have you acted more like a slave or God's child?

The parable of the lost son in Luke 15:11–32 depicts both the son and slave mentalities. The parable tells of a father who has two sons. The younger son leaves and squanders his inheritance but then decides to humbly return to his father. He offers to become his dad's servant to repay him. But his dad is not mad; rather, he is thrilled that his son has come home. With compassion, the father throws a homecoming celebration, and his son is adorned with new clothes, shoes, and a ring. The son, now bestowed with grace, maintains his status as a son and does not need to become his father's slave.

Meanwhile, the older brother discovers the reason for the party and becomes offended. Anger burns inside him, and he refuses to join in the festivities, saying, "Look! All these years I've been *slaving* for you and never disobeyed your orders. Yet you never gave me even a young goat so I could celebrate with my friends."[171] The dad responds, "My son, you are always with me, and everything I have is yours."

In the same way, we, as God's children, are always with Him, and everything He has is ours. When we live in shame, however, we take on a slave mentality. This mentality keeps us from receiving all that our heavenly Father desires to give to us as His sons and daughters, and we forfeit what is rightfully ours.

As I learned these lessons in my own walk with God, my slave identity gradually returned to that of being God's daughter. I no longer tried to earn my identity by being legalistic; I simply rested in the security of my Father's love, knowing I belonged in His family. And the more I lived *from* the position of having God's approval as His daughter, the more I became free to be me.

Today I know that I am special simply because God loves and accepts me unconditionally. My significance comes from being His daughter, and I find my value and identity in Christ, based on who God is and my belonging to Him. I'm important because God says so, and He proved it by sending His one and only Son to die on my behalf.

> How different would your life look if you lived from a position of rest, knowing you already have your heavenly Father's acceptance?

## Where is Your "House" Built?

It's not unusual to place our significance and identity in our career, appearance, ministry, parenting, or marriage, but the truth is we have little control over these things and they can change in a moment. We see this idea play out in the parable of the wise and foolish builders in Matthew 7:24–27. The wise builder listens and obeys the Word; thus, his house is built on the rock. When the rains come and the winds blow, hammering against the house, it does not fall. Likewise, when we have personal storms — when our career or ministry fails, when we lose our appearance to age, or when we become empty-nesters or have marital discord — we will remain stable if the foundation of our "house" (our identity) is built on the rock of Christ. Having our identity securely fastened to Christ, the One who does not change and who will never leave or forsake us, prevents us from being tossed about in the storms of life.

In what or whom have you placed your identity?

Our significance and identity in Christ are permanent. They are not affected by success or failure, sin or holiness. They are consistent because they revolve around the steadfast truths of *who we are* (our Father's children) and *whose we are* (God's), and not around what we do.

Ask the Lord to reveal your identity — who He says you are. Write it down.

## Staking Our Claim

*Now we're no longer living like slaves under the law, but we enjoy being God's very own sons and daughters! And because we're his, we can access everything our Father has — for we are heirs of God through Jesus, the Messiah!*

GALATIANS 4:7 (TPT)

Inheritance is "a possession to which one has received the legal claim." As sons and daughters of Christ, our inheritance, which cannot perish, spoil, or fade, includes the following:

- The hope of eternal life
- The role of priests reigning on earth
- Redemption and forgiveness of sins
- Deliverance from darkness
- Security in Christ

Inheritance also speaks to our destiny. It is the Promised Land — our life's destiny — to which the Father wants to deliver us. And it is our position as co-heirs with Christ, in which everything that is His is ours as well.

But destiny needs to be stepped into. We don't just sit back and watch our destiny fall into our lap; it must be pursued before it is fulfilled. And the pursuit, in this case, means becoming who we're born to be.

After my earthly dad passed, for example, a portion of his inheritance rightfully belonged to me; but I wasn't able to receive my portion until I proved my true identity as his daughter. In the same way, in order to receive everything that God has intended for me, I must acknowledge my position as His child and have faith that everything He says about me is true. And then I must step into that position, declaring my true identity and living it out. So when God tells me I will "mentor the masses," I must have faith in His word and step into this identity by writing a weekly blog post and mentoring women one-on-one.

And what about you? The following is a partial list from Neil Anderson's *Victory Over Darkness* about what we can rightfully claim as heirs of God. I encourage you to step out in faith, declare these truths aloud, and thus step into your true identity as Christ's beloved:

- I am a child of God.[172]
- I am God's workmanship.[173]
- I am a citizen of heaven, seated in heaven right now.[174]
- I am a new creation.[175]
- I am Christ's friend.[176]
- I am righteous and holy.[177]
- I am chosen by God, holy and dearly loved.[178]
- I am a saint.[179]

How can you grab hold of your inheritance in Christ? Declare who you are in Christ on a daily basis.

. . . . . . . . . . . . . . . . . . . . . . . .

## What I Heard My Father Say

*My child, let me give you a new name. Allow me to create within you the person I have made you to be. Don't listen to the father of lies or let him steal your identity. Dwell upon my truth about who you really are: Your past sin doesn't define your future inheritance; I will redeem all that for your good and my glory. The person I made you to be is enough. And your worth and significance will never fade based on any work that you can do. Place your identity in me and in who I say you are as my child. Embrace your inheritance and step into your destiny.*

**Take time to wait before the Lord.**
**Ask Him what He wants to say to you regarding this chapter.**

# ~ The Heart of the Matter ~

- Until we *see* ourselves as God does, we won't *be* who He created.
- We struggle with seeing ourselves through God's eyes because of the lies we believe.
- If we haven't fully received God's forgiveness for the sins in our past, then we won't be able to move forward in freedom.
- We are not who our past says we are; we are who God says we are.
- God gives us new names to reveal our true identity — who we will become if we believe.
- God's love for us is based on who He is and on what Jesus did for us on the cross, not on how well we obey Him.
- There is nothing we could ever do or say to make God love us more or less than He already does.
- Our past doesn't define our future; rather, our past is used by God to equip us for our destiny.
- Our actions are the fruit of the lies and truths we have agreed with and believed.
- Our identity is based not on what we think or on what others think; it's clarified through God's eyes and what He thinks about us.
- God doesn't want us to primarily live our lives doing things for Him; He simply wants us to be with Him.
- Our identity is stolen by the devil when we don't see ourselves as God does or agree with His view of us.
- Our actions align with our beliefs about our identity.
- God's not asking us to be like someone else. He's only asking us to be who He has created us to be.
- Comparison kills who we really are and who God made us to be.

- When we believe we are slaves, we forfeit what is rightfully ours.
- Destiny needs to be stepped into.
- Our identity in Christ is permanent and gives us stability during the storms of life.
- The more I live from the position of having God's approval as His child, the more I am free to be me.
- We can't do anything to become what we already are — God's children.

# — 9 —
# BEING IN THE PRESENCE OF GOD

*Whoever dwells in the shelter of the Most High*
*will rest in the shadow of the Almighty.*

PSALM 91:1

Intimacy with God involves, first and foremost, knowing God, which leads to everything else — trusting, loving, and obeying Him and living fully alive in our identity as His child. But how exactly do we achieve that first step? That is, how do we *really* get to know God? In the chapter "Knowing God," we discussed why it's important to know who God is experientially, how misperceptions and truths about God affect the way we relate to Him, and how getting to know God requires us to pursue Him with our time, communication, experience, and commitment. Now we turn to practical tools you can use to get to know God better: "soaking" (in this chapter) and listening to His voice (in the next chapter). These tools will especially help you to experience God's presence.

Being in God's presence is beneficial for us. His name Immanuel, meaning "God with us," speaks to the truth that God continually sees us, pursues us, and wants to spend time with us, just as He did when He walked in the garden looking for Adam and Eve.[180] But God wants us to be the ones to seek and spend time in His presence, as this is evidence of our love and need for Him.

To see this more clearly, let's revisit God's meeting with Moses on Mount Sinai. When Moses goes up to the mountain, a pillar of cloud descends as "the glory of the Lord settled on Mount Sinai."[181] When Moses is delayed in returning, however, the Israelites grow impatient and ask Aaron to make them other gods to serve. Both the Lord and Moses are understandably angered by the Israelites' rebellion, as it puts a breach in the people's relationship with God. Yet Moses, to help mend the breach, pitches a tent "outside the camp some distance away" and calls it the "tent of meeting."[182] The tent is a temporary place where the people can go meet with the Lord, and whenever Moses enters it, the pillar of cloud comes down, hovering at the entrance, and the Lord speaks to Moses "face to face, as a man speaks with his friend."[183]

Like Moses, if we want to be in the presence of God, we must go after it. We must be the ones who initiate and make effort to seek God out. We must walk out of our camp, go somewhere beyond the comforts we enjoy, and find the "place" where God's presence is. The ball is in our court.

I am grateful that, even when we sin, God provides us with such a place, because He wants our relationship to be restored. He gives us a tent of meeting — a way to come into His presence and return to Him. And whoever is willing to seek the Lord will be welcomed and find Him.

## One Thing

*One thing I ask from the Lord, this only do I*
*seek: that I may dwell in the house of the Lord*
*all the days of my life, to gaze on the beauty*
*of the Lord and to seek him in his temple.*

PSALM 27:4

In Exodus 33:13, Moses reveals to God his main motives for seeking out and spending time in God's presence: "If you are pleased with me, *teach me your ways* so I may *know you* and continue to *find favor with you* [emphasis mine]." Following in Moses's footsteps, we can also seek out the presence of God in order to learn His ways, to know Him, and to find His favor.

- **To learn God's ways.** In Isaiah 55:8, God says, "For my thoughts are not your thoughts, neither are your ways my ways." When we spend time in God's presence, we can better understand His heart.

- **To know God.** Philippians 3:10 says, "I want to know Christ — yes, to know the power of his resurrection and participation in his sufferings, becoming like him in his death."[184] When we seek to be in God's presence, we demonstrate that our desire to know Him personally is greater than our desire for anything He might promise us. Said another way, we show that we want the Giver more than the gifts He can give.

- **To find favor with God.** James 4:8a says, "Come near to God, and he will come near to you." When we seek to be near God, He draws near to us, revealing His heart and His approval of us.

Later in the story of Moses, we see that Moses feels so secure in his relationship with God that he boldly asks God to show him His glory.[185] God's glory consists of encountering His goodness, declaring His name, and experiencing His grace, mercy, and compassion.[186] In this instance, however, Moses is asking God to show Himself physically. God, in His kindness, answers Moses's prayer, but knowing that Moses won't be able to physically live after seeing His face, the Lord hides Moses in the cleft of a rock. When God's glory passes by, He covers Moses with His hand so that Moses can see only God's back.[187]

I appreciate how Moses wasn't content with his relationship with God; he always wanted more of God's presence. It wasn't enough for Moses to see the cloud by day and the pillar of fire by night. It wasn't enough to hear God's voice. He wanted more, so he pleaded with God to show him His glory. Matthew Henry wrote this about Moses: "The more he had, the more he asked." He went on to write, "All that are effectually called to the knowledge of God and fellowship with Him, though they desire nothing more than God, are nevertheless still coveting more and more of Him, till they come to see as they are seen."

Moses valued being in God's presence over everything else. In fact, God's presence was so important to Moses, he told God that if His presence didn't go with them, he didn't want to leave.[188] He couldn't imagine moving forward without God.

May we become like Moses — refusing to proceed without God's presence in our life, refusing to be content with where our relationship with God is today, and always hungering and thirsting to be more intimate with the Lover of our soul.

 Is God's presence that important to you? What will you sacrifice to spend time with God?

When we are desperate and really want something, we will go after it no matter what. It doesn't matter how foolish we may look or what man may think. No sacrifice is too great. The Bible is full of examples of those whose faith was put into action because they loved the Lord. Jacob wrestled with the angel of the Lord.[189] Blind Bartimaeus got louder, seeking the attention of Jesus when those near him rebuked him and told him to be quiet.[190] David didn't fear looking foolish when he danced before the Lord after the ark of the covenant was returned to Jerusalem.[191] The woman who'd been bleeding for twelve years pressed through the crowds in desperation just to touch the hem of Jesus's garment and be healed.[192] God loves it when we become so desperate for Him that we have to have Him.

I experienced a desperation like this on our first visit to the Brownsville revival in Florida during the late nineties. I felt compelled by God to go up and have Dr. Michael Brown pray for me after one of his sessions, for an anointing in writing. At the beginning of his talk, however, he had mentioned he would not be able to pray for anyone after his session because he had a plane to catch. Normally I am submissive to authority, but my faith for this was about to burst, and I knew I had to obey God!

As soon as Dr. Brown finished his message, I darted out of the pew and ran up to him. Little did I know the ushers were coming up the aisle to stop me. I tapped Dr. Brown on his arm and asked him to pray for an anointing to write. I have no idea what he said, though, because the next thing I knew, I was lying on the ground, having been slain in the Spirit. That's the kind of faith and hunger God delights in: the kind that says that His presence and anointing is what we have to have and that He alone will satisfy.

Just as God met with Moses, He wants to meet with you! And just as He did with Moses, when we seek His presence, He answers. So, go after the presence of God with all you have, totally abandoned to God with a surrendered heart. Be like Moses and seek to learn God's ways, know God, and to find favor with Him. Tell God "whatever, whenever, however, I am yours."

Describe a time when you were desperate for God's presence.

# Soaking 101

*My soul waits for the Lord more than*
*watchmen wait for the morning, more*
*than watchmen wait for the morning.*

PSALM 130:6 (RSV)

One way we can abandon ourselves to God and show our great affection for Him is through a practice called soaking. The dictionary definition of *soak* is "to lie immersed; to become saturated by or as if by immersion." Here the immersion we're talking about comes when we are fully saturated in the Holy Spirit. Imagine immersing a dry sponge into a sink of water. Likewise, when we soak with the Lord, we immerse ourselves and become filled with the Holy Spirit. When used in this sense, the word *soak* can be remembered as an acronym: SOAK — Simple Outrageous Abandonment to the King.

In practice, soaking is simply asking the Holy Spirit to invade every part of our being, and then waiting on or resting in His presence. It reminds me of when John and I were teenagers living in Phoenix. We would lay out by the pool and soak in the sun. Soaking in the Son is a similar experience. It involves simply lying still and doing nothing, except for seeking and resting in Him.

When we choose to soak, we're telling God we want to have time alone with Him. We're deciding to *be* with God rather than to *do* for Him. We're not expecting anything from God, and He is not expecting anything from us. It's a "date" with God, when we can experience unconditional intimacy with one another.

 In what ways are the above thoughts new to you?

## The Nuts and Bolts of Soaking

The practice of soaking reminds me of the practice of jogging: it takes little equipment and can be done almost anywhere or at any time. I usually lay on the floor under a blanket and listen to worship music or something instrumental. I quietly tell the Lord I love Him, want Him, and have to have Him. I surrender all of my heart to Him and ask the Holy Spirit to possess me. I ask Him to take total control over my mind, will, and emotions and to make me one with Him. Then the last thing I usually say is, "Cause me to fall more madly in love with you!"

When I first learned about soaking and heard about the soaking rooms at women's conferences, I avoided it because it seemed mystical and "too out there." Plus, the idea of just lying in wait for God went against my upbringing, which had instilled in me the idea that I must always be busy to be productive. But eventually, I was invited to my friend's house to soak, so I tried it. At first, my inner mind had difficultly quieting itself as thoughts bombarded me. But eventually, I got into a "zone," which I now describe as a state of being half awake and half asleep. The peace of God enveloped me and I sensed His love for me wash over me, drawing me closer to His heart. I was hooked. After that, I decided to try to make soaking a regular personal practice.

My consistency in soaking paid off. Over time, I could more quickly get into the zone, sometimes even falling asleep, which I discovered was fine and no reason to feel guilty. Rarely did I experience what some might call "Holy Spirit feelings," such as goosebumps or tingling on my arms or neck, although sometimes I experienced warmth, as if He were wrapping me up in a blanket. Other times, I experienced His peace, comfort, rest, and encouragement upon me, and my breathing and heart rate slowed down. But often, I felt no different. And I learned that was okay too.

In fact, since those beginnings, I have learned several things about soaking. I have discovered that when I don't feel anything while soaking, the enemy can make me feel condemned or ashamed about that, which only leads to frustration or striving. But soaking should not be about feelings; it should be simply about seeking the presence of God. As C. S. Lewis wrote in *Letters to an American Lady*, "It is the actual presence, not the sensation of the presence, of the Holy Ghost which begets Christ in us."

I have also found that my mind is easily distracted, so I now prepare to soak by making sure I have a paper and pen nearby. I jot down distracting thoughts as they come, which puts them out of my mind's bandwidth and onto a hard copy. As a bonus, I can write down any words He speaks to me as I soak.

Finally, I have learned that Jesus wants me to come as I am, even with all of my imperfections and sin. One time I avoided soaking because of my struggle with a sin issue. I thought I needed to be spiritually cleansed before

I could meet with Him. But He encouraged me to soak with Him anyway. He said, *"That's the time to come!"* God knew that what was best for me was not to hide from Him with my sin and shame but to come to Him as I am. The Lord knew that soaking would wet and soften the soil of my heart and that His kindness would lead me to repentance and a restored relationship with Him. And that is exactly what happened.

The concept of soaking may be new to you. Intimidating, even. But simply look at it as another way to enter into God's presence, a place where you can be with Jesus, growing closer to Him. It doesn't matter how or where. It's not a performance. It's a way to pursue an intimate relationship with God. What matters is that you're intentional and make it a habit to enter the secret place and that, like Moses, you value finding the presence of God. God's waiting to meet with you. What are you waiting for?

> Do you have experience with soaking? Practice soaking for five minutes. Turn on worship music and be still. Let God's peace and rest quiet you.

## The Purpose of Soaking

*Be still, and know that I am God.*

PSALM 46:10A

The primary purpose of soaking is **to deepen our intimacy with God.** When we choose to set aside our time and attention for Jesus through soaking, we're choosing our relationship with Him over everything else vying for our time or attention (whether people or activities). It's an expression of our love and need for God. In essence, we're saying to Him, "You're my priority. I have to be with you!"

I believe quality time is God's favorite love language. He wants to hold the position of primary importance within our hearts and desires to become our resting place. And when we prioritize Him in this way, it changes our life. In fact, I went through a season when it seemed I was "addicted" to soaking. I just had to spend more time in the presence of God, because it was changing my life! I discovered, however, that it's not soaking that changes your life but rather the intimacy with God that comes as a result of soaking. Soaking and intimacy go hand in hand. You can't consistently soak without intimacy with the Lord eventually happening. Yet, we can't take any credit because when we lay on the floor to soak, we are doing absolutely nothing!

We also soak as a way **to surrender to God.** We abandon ourselves to Him or give ourselves up to His control and influence, letting the Holy Spirit come upon and settle deep within us. As a result, more of us becomes more of His, and we belong more to Him than to ourselves. As Andrew Murray writes, "He wants to be wholly our possession, that we may be wholly his possession."

Abandoning ourselves to God in this way results in a sense of becoming one with God and experiencing a secret place of divine union. This is the place I desire — the place where the lines become blurred, where people can't tell where I end and the Lord begins and our oneness solidifies.

Such unity allows us a greater revelation of who God is and a greater understanding of what makes His heart beat. When this happens, we become more attached to God and "rooted and established in love... to grasp how wide and long and high and deep is the love of Christ... that you may be filled to the measure of all the fullness of God."*193*

Based on the purposes mentioned above, why would you want to soak?

## Hindrances to Soaking

*A voice of one calling: "In the wilderness*
*prepare the way for the Lord; make straight*
*in the desert a highway for our God."*

ISAIAH 40:3

Satan does not want us to spend time being still with God, so he will place obstacles in our path to try to keep us from soaking. One of the biggest obstacles is **feeling obligated to "do" rather than just "be."** As mentioned, this was one of my biggest obstacles before I even started soaking. The idea of doing nothing but just lying in wait for God went against the lie I'd believed that I must be doing something in order to be productive. But after time, I realized that what we often deem as unproductive might just be the most productive use of our time in God's economy. Isaiah 55:8 informs us that God's thoughts and ways are not ours, and, indeed, you don't have to be a Christian for long to realize that the kingdom of God holds a viewpoint that usually seems upside-down from the world's. From the world's point of view, although soaking may appear to be a waste of time, it is really an investment into the greatest intimate relationship we could ever have, which affects all other relationships and areas of life. Even David, the "man after God's own heart," recognized the value of being still in God's presence.

**Distractions** also keep us from resting in God's presence. Because I have attention deficit disorder, my mind can bounce from one thought to another, especially when it comes to my to-do list. When I taught fourth grade, the beginning of the year was especially difficult for me as I began to set up my classroom. I'd be putting up a bulletin board when I'd remember something else I had to do. So I'd stop what I was doing to start the new project, only to be distracted yet again by another task that needed my attention. It took me forever to get my classroom set up because of my lack of focus. Likewise, when I soak, sometimes my mind has difficulty slowing its pace and settling down to focus on just being in God's presence. After regularly practicing soaking for some time, however, my mind has become more accustomed to settling down and can do so more quickly. And as mentioned in the previous section, my paper and pen are always at the ready, awaiting download of any distracting thoughts.

**Intellect** can get in the way of soaking as well. When we lay in the presence of God, our communication with Him is Spirit-to-spirit which involves our faith, not our intellect. So instead of analyzing why or how we are soaking, for example, we need to simply jump in and do it, experiencing it firsthand. Think of it like testing the integrity of a chair. If I want to know whether a chair will hold me, I can intellectually analyze it, looking at the materials it's made of or assessing its construction to see how well it's put together. But it's my sitting on the chair that is the true test, both of its integrity and my faith.

Finally, we must remember from part 1 of this book that intimacy with God is often made possible only by healing from hurts such as **detachment,**

**rejection, shame, fear,** and **lies**. Therefore, holding onto these hurts is a natural obstacle that can prevent us from soaking. If you're still struggling with any of these hurts, I encourage you to go back through part one to revisit how you can partner with God to heal your heart.

Which of these hindrances prevent you from spending time in God's presence?

## The Beauty of Soaking

*Yes, my soul, find rest in God; my hope comes from him.*

PSALM 62:5

When we overcome our obstacles to invest in our relationship with Jesus through soaking, we make deposits into our spiritual relationship, which, in time, will pay great dividends. Our commitment to having time alone with the Lover of our souls will bring a return on our investment that we will not regret.

Chief among the returns we will receive is **greater intimacy with and knowledge of God,** which is achieved through various avenues:

- **We bond with God in a way that allows us to experience His permanency.** Through soaking, we can form an attachment to Him that teaches us He is always there for us, even when we don't see Him. It's like the idea of *relational object constancy* in child psychology: only when children's brains reach a certain stage of maturity do they develop the ability "to remember that people or objects are consistent, trustworthy and reliable, especially when they are out of your immediate field of vision."

- **We feel a oneness with God, which brings a sense of mutual knowing and understanding.** When we soak, it's as if a divine union takes place, which deepens our experiential knowledge of God. Greater understanding of God's unconditional love for and acceptance of us enters our hearts. In turn, we realize that we are also known by God. Entering God's "secret place," the Holy Spirit gives us revelation, by which we discover who He is, who we are (our identity), and the plans He has for us, fulfilling God's promise in Isaiah 45:3: "I will give you hidden treasures, riches stored in secret places, so that you may know that I am the Lord, the God of Israel, who summons you by name."

- **We gain authority or credibility.** Our authority increases through the knowledge we've obtained while in God's secret place. Recently, God spoke these words to me: *Authority comes as you spend time in the secret place with me. The surer you are of who I am, the surer you are of yourself. You don't doubt who I am and won't doubt who you are. Authority is a result of believing and trusting who I am and who I've created you to be.*

In addition to bringing intimacy with God, soaking **renews our mind, will, and emotions**:

- **The Holy Spirit downloads truth to our mind.** I have found one of the best ways to prepare for writing a message is by soaking before I sit down to write, so that His thoughts become my thoughts, poured out on the page.

- **The Holy Spirit communicates with our spirit and takes greater possession of our hearts.** As I become saturated with God's presence, my heart becomes more captured by Him. And when He has my heart, He has all of me, because as the heart goes, so goes the person. As King Solomon penned in Proverbs 4:23, "Above all else, guard your heart, for everything you do flows from it." When He has our heart and spirit, we sin less because we desire to please the One we love.

- **We experience quietness of mind, and our spirit is refreshed and filled.** Augustine of Hippo wrote, "Our hearts are restless, until they can find rest in you." Soaking is a place of refuge for me, often producing peace, satisfaction, and contentment that settle my soul, fulfilling God's promises that "He satisfies the thirsty and fills the hungry with good things"[194] and "He makes me lie down in green pastures, he leads me beside quiet waters, he refreshes my soul."[195] Even when I am finished soaking, I experience fulfillment of God's promise that "My Presence will go with you, and I will give you rest."[196]

- **We find emotional healing and restoration.** Soaking is a place where I can find God's comfort and strength. And the more I receive comfort from Him, the less I seek counterfeit comfort in the form of idols. One time, when I had been deeply emotionally wounded by a loved one, I got down on the floor and covered myself with a blanket, ready to soak. The Holy Spirit comforted me as it says in 2 Corinthians 1:3–5. It was as if I was snuggled up on my Father God's lap, and He hugged me, stroking the hair on the back of my head. He said, "*It's okay, my precious daughter. Pour out your heart and hurts to me. Get it all out and let me comfort you.*" I did just that. I sobbed and sobbed and got it all out. God comforted me and set me free from my emotional pain and restored my heart.

- **Our closer friendship with God dispels feelings of loneliness and rejection.** Jude 21a says, "Keep yourselves in God's love…" As my intimacy with God deepens by spending time soaking in His presence, I not only maintain myself in God's love but also become more secure in it. As a result, I become less reliant on the love of others. I became aware of this when we moved to Wichita after living in Omaha for twenty-eight years. Even though I missed my family and friends, I didn't experience loneliness. My nearness to God had developed to the point where I wasn't lonely, even though I was alone.

Lastly, during our times of soaking, God is **anointing us to minister**. Imagine immersing a dry sponge into a sink of water. The sponge becomes so full of liquid that, when you take it from the sink, you must squeeze out the excess. Likewise, when we soak with the Lord, we become so filled with the Holy Spirit that we must pour Him back out to others. For this reason, I sometimes soak in preparation for writing or speaking. I know that if I'm full of the Holy Spirit, He will inevitably spill out onto my readers, audience, or anyone else I come in contact with. As Julian of Norwich says, "This inner rest is the very thing that makes it possible for Him to flood us with the power of grace — pouring Himself into us and out to others through us."

Which of the beauties of soaking motivates you to want to soak? Take ten to twenty minutes to enter into God's presence through soaking.

. . . . . . . . . . . . . . . . . . . . . . . . .

## What I Heard My Father Say

*Enter my presence, my child, as you are. Let "being" with me foster our oneness. Divine union comes as a result of spending time alone together. I value your desire to be with me more than what you do for me. It's all about deepening our relationship. And through the process of your being in my presence, I equip you for ministry. Choose time alone with me. You won't be disappointed.*

**Take time to wait before the Lord.
Ask Him what He wants to say to you regarding this chapter.**

## ~ The Heart of the Matter ~

- When you've tasted the presence of the Lord, you don't want to leave.
- Becoming one with God and experiencing the secret place of divine union occurs when we're being still in God's presence.
- Being in the presence of God is a form of "being," not "doing."
- The greater our intimacy with God becomes, the less we'll seek intimacy with counterfeit lovers such as idols.
- God is anointing us to minister as we spend time in His presence.
- When we intentionally spend time in God's presence, we become more attached to God and realize that, even though we don't see Him, He is there for us, and He is consistent, trustworthy, and reliable.
- Being still in God's presence is powerful because it chooses relationship over religion.
- Quality time is God's favorite love language.

# — 10 —
# "SPEAK LORD, YOUR SERVANT IS LISTENING"

*My sheep listen to my voice; I know them, and they follow me.*

JOHN 10:27

Listening to God's voice has been a learning process for me. The first time I tried it was in 1999, when the speaker at a women's retreat directed us to sit still before the Lord to hear His voice. I went outside, sat on a boulder, and watched an ant walk by. I heard nothing, except the distractions in my mind, bouncing back and forth like a ping-pong ball.

Since then, I have had to learn how to sit still and quiet my mind to hear God's voice. And I have come to understand why Mother Theresa said, "Listen in silence because if your heart is full of other things, you cannot hear the voice of God." Like anything else, the more I practice this silent listening, the easier it gets. The more time I spend with God, the better I know Him; and the better I know Him, the clearer His voice is and the more frequently He speaks. By now, my ears have tuned into the same frequency as His voice; I have heard it while making my husband's lunch, putting on my makeup, cleaning the house, and dancing in Zumba class.

In general, God speaks when He knows we're willing to listen and obey. The more our ears are trained to hear His voice, the more often we'll hear it, even when we're not expecting it.

 How have you struggled with hearing God's voice?

# Why God Speaks

*We proclaim to you what we have seen and*
*heard, so that you may also have fellowship*
*with us. And our fellowship is with the*
*Father and with His Son, Jesus Christ.*

1 JOHN 1:3

The primary reason God speaks is **to build an intimate relationship with us.** God is all about relationships. And all relationships are built and deepened by communication. For example, my husband and I have been married for over forty years. What would our relationship be like if we rarely talked with each other and never shared our hearts? Or what if we had a one-way relationship, where I was the only one doing the talking? One-way communication is not conducive to a healthy relationship; rather, intimate two-way relationships need two-way communication, with both parties talking and listening. Our relationship with God is no different: listening to God is as important as talking to Him.

Hearing and obeying God's voice has caused my relationship with Him to grow more than any other spiritual discipline. In fact, my intimacy with God increased by leaps and bounds when I became intentional in sitting still to listen to His voice and to journal what I heard Him say. This practice has been life-changing! One of the worst things God could ever do is to stop speaking to me.

Listening to God can build intimacy in our relationship in three primary ways:

1. **We discover how well He knows and loves us.** And when we do, our attachment to God deepens, causing our loneliness to disappear. Dr. Curt Thompson, in *Anatomy of the Soul,* says God wants us to have this discovery: "While he desires for us to have the experience of being known by him, just as important is his desire to experience being known by us."

2. **We discover more about who He is.** We hear His heart; we connect with how He feels and what He thinks; and we discover what He loves and what displeases Him. I agree with Shawn Bolz, when he says in his book *Translating God,*

He reveals His secrets to humanity because He treats us all as friends. God is speaking to everyone who wants to listen, but He only has ongoing, long-term conversations with His friends. As His sons and daughters, He is more interested in communicating so that we do things with Him rather than for Him.

In the same way that we typically share the recesses of our hearts only with friends, so, too, does God reserve His secrets for those who are closest to Him. We see evidence of this in Psalm 25:14 (TPT), which says, "There's a private place reserved for the lovers of God, where they sit near him and receive the revelation-secrets of his promises." We also see this in Genesis 22, when, as a result of Abraham hearing and obeying God's voice over and over again, God reveals Himself to Abraham in a new way: as *Jehovah Jireh*, "the Lord will provide." In the same way, each time we listen and obey God's voice, we gain understanding of another facet of God's nature, and our relationship with Him deepens. I love to listen to God speak, because it's a way I get to know my heavenly Daddy, and as a result, my trust in Him grows. In turn, the more I trust Him, the more intimate we become.

3. **We discover God's desire to connect with us**. When we hear God's voice, we experience firsthand His demonstration of the three characteristics of attachment: presence or proximity, attentiveness, and responsiveness. These characteristics anchor our security in God and deepen our relationship with Him. One day, in a Zumba class, I heard the Lord say, *"Don't look at hearing my voice as if it's one more thing a taskmaster is requiring you to do. Look at it from the viewpoint of a husband or a lover who simply loves you and longs to be with you, to share His heart with you."* Hearing God say this in the middle of a dance class, when I least expected it, displayed to me His availability and desire to connect with me.

Besides speaking to build intimacy, God speaks **to give us direction and answer our questions**. "Whether you turn to the right or to the left, your ears will hear a voice behind you, saying, 'This is the way; walk in it.'"[197] Figuring out God's will for our lives may seem mysterious, but it's an opportunity to have God explain what He desires for each of us.

My husband and I lived in Tucson, Arizona for sixteen years, during which time we went to college and graduate school. John's final year of training moved us to Chicago. I dealt with our move okay because I knew beyond a shadow of a doubt that we would return to a job in Tucson. Our fifth month in Chicago brought us to a crossroads, however, as a job opportunity opened up in Omaha, Nebraska. I wrestled with God, and my husband and I began to ask God what He wanted us to do. Then, while John was interviewing in Omaha and I was in Chicago taking care of our kids, God gave the same Scripture verse to both of us: "The Lord had said to Abram, 'Go from your country, your people and your father's household to the land I will show you.'"[198] One translation reads, "Go to the land you know not of." Omaha was definitely a place we knew nothing about! God had answered our prayer for direction by giving us this verse.

God wants us to ask Him questions and to get our marching orders from Him: "Call to me and I will answer you and tell you great and unsearchable things you do not know."[199] There is no question He can't answer.

> Sit still before the Lord to seek His answers to your questions and to get His direction for your life.

Thirdly, God speaks **to warn us**. He does this in many ways, but for Joseph, the earthly father of Jesus, God spoke through angels in Joseph's dreams. The first time this happened, in Matthew 1:20–21, an angel directed Joseph to espouse Mary and receive confirmation of her pregnancy by the Holy Spirit. Later, the angel appeared again to Joseph in a dream, instructing him to escape to Egypt and warning him that Herod was trying to kill his son, Jesus.[200] A few verses later, we see Joseph receiving word to go to the land of Israel.[201]

Lastly, God speaks **to birth new life and possibilities within us**. God's voice restores, heals, comforts, and shows us our destiny and purpose in life. Author and prophetess Lana Vawser writes, "When the Lord speaks, his voice creates and establishes. His words shift our reality and bring us into His reality." God wants to encourage us with the words He speaks to us.

In my own life, the new names God spoke over me (Mary, Daddy's Girl, Queen, and Bride) showed me my identity and called out who I was to become, breathing life into me and setting me on a new life course. Then in 2000, the Lord said that one day I would "mentor the masses," and mentoring in the areas of emotional healing and deepening intimacy with God has been my focus ever since.

Our pastors in Wichita say, "One word from God changes everything." This is so true. Wonderful blessings result from hearing God's voice, which comes as we spend time in His presence. Keep in mind, however, that no one likes to be desired only for what they give. My closest friends, for example, are those who enjoy being with me — not those who want something from me. I believe God is the same way. As you seek to hear God's voice, then, I encourage you to be aware of your motivation for doing so. In your time of listening, seek to know and be with God and not just get something from Him. Seek the Giver more than His gifts.

> When have you heard God's voice? What were some of the reasons He spoke to you?

## How God Speaks

*And afterward, I will pour out my Spirit on all people. Your sons and daughters will prophesy, your old men will dream dreams, your young men will see visions.*

JOEL 2:28

God speaks to each of us in various ways. In fact, for this reason, I have come to understand that people often hear God's voice more than they realize. The misconception is that God's voice must be like a man's deep, booming voice, when more often than not, it isn't. Rather, God's voice often sounds like our own, which is why many discount it, believing it is their thoughts instead of discerning it as God speaking to them.

I have never heard God's voice audibly, although I know some people have. A few times, His words were so emphatic, however, that I thought they were spoken out loud, such as when He said, *"Mentor the masses"* and when He told me that He had created me for greatness. Most often, though, I hear His voice in my head, and it usually sounds like mine. It is a gentle whisper or **a still, small voice**, like the one He used with the prophet Elijah in 1 Kings 19:12. It's as if I'm wearing an earpiece, through which He whispers His thoughts to me. He'll give me one word or phrase, and as I write it down in my journal, He'll continue to speak more. Sentence upon sentence and paragraph upon paragraph, I record what God says, like a secretary taking shorthand from my Boss.

At times, **I see a ticker tape** of His words going across my mind like an airplane advertising a message. God has also **quickened Scripture** within me, as He did with our move to Omaha. It's as if a verse jumps out at me. I also have **impressions,** or gut-level feelings, about something, as if **I have a "knowing."**

God has given me **word pictures** for others as well. I will sit quietly before the Lord when I'm writing in a loved one's birthday card, waiting for a word from Him to encourage them. One time when I asked Him what He wanted to say to a girlfriend of mine; He showed me a picture of a pearl necklace while stopped at a red light. Another time, when God wanted to confirm our move to Wichita, I saw His hand on our backs, pushing us out of Omaha. When I get a word picture, I ask God what it means and what I'm supposed to do with it. For instance, when I asked the Lord His meaning behind the string of pearls, He reminded me of how pearls are formed in oysters. When an irritant invades an oyster, there is a defense mechanism fluid that covers the irritant. The multiple protective layers of fluid eventually form a beautiful pearl. Likewise, the pain my friend had walked through, had formed within her beautiful "pearls" of godly attributes.

Often, **dreams** of a spiritual nature will stay with me throughout the day, returning to my thoughts, sometimes in great detail. When this happens, I seek God's clarification or interpretation of the dreams.

Finally, I will get **visions**, which are like dreams but happen when we're wide awake and our eyes are open. It's like I'm watching a movie on a screen right in front of me. I don't get those very often, so when I do, I pay close attention. The most recent one I had took place in Wichita in 2015. This was before my move to Wichita, but a group of girlfriends and I had driven there to attend a Beth Moore conference. During worship, I had a vision of myself in the shallow end of a swimming pool, and Jesus stood in front of me. He turned to grab my hand and started to walk toward the deep end of the pool. I was never a hundred percent sure of its meaning, but I find it interesting that I now live in Wichita!

Sometimes, when I question whether it's His voice I'm hearing, He will confirm His word by giving it to me a few times. It's like a broken record that I hear over and over. Recently, on a flight to Chicago, I had a conversation with the woman who sat next to me. Then I began to read my book, and the Holy Spirit whispered, *"Pray for her."* I continued to read, but He nudged me two more times to put down the book and to pray for her. As a result of God's persistence, I gave up trying to read the chapter until after I obeyed Him. I closed my book, turned to her, and asked her if I could pray for her. She willingly said yes.

God places His ideas into our hearts in all of these ways.[202] And the more you get to know God, through reading his Word and seeing how He operates in your life, the less you will question whose voice you're hearing.

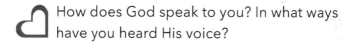 How does God speak to you? In what ways have you heard His voice?

## Obstacles to Hearing God's Voice

*So is my word that goes out from my mouth: It will not return to me empty, but will accomplish what I desire and achieve the purpose for which I sent it.*

ISAIAH 55:11

One thing is for sure: the enemy does not want us to hear God's voice, so he sets up roadblocks to prevent us from listening. One of the first obstacles I experienced was **distractions**. My attention deficit disorder made it initially difficult to sit still. This is not an uncommon experience, though.

Even Oswald Chambers wrote, "What hinders me from hearing is my attention to other things." This is exactly what Satan desires — for our focus to be on anything other than God.

But I've learned that this is another good opportunity to put my pen and paper to use. I already have them next to me to record anything I hear from God. So if my thoughts distract me, I jot them down, leaving me with a clear mind to hear God speak.

Another thing that helps is to remember these words that God comforted me with once: *"It doesn't bother me, Norma, if your mind bounces around when you're trying to sit still and hear my voice. What matters more is that you want to spend time alone with me. Seeing your heart's desire is what counts most."*

> What practical steps can you take to help overcome distractions?

Another hindrance to hearing God's voice is **not making it a priority**. We see this all throughout the book of Isaiah. God is appealing to the Israelites, whom He had just freed from exile, to listen to Him, to trust Him, and to return their hearts to Him. Even though the Israelites are following Levitical sacrifices and offerings, their hearts are far from God and they trust only in themselves. It is as if they are paying lip service to God. So, through the prophet Isaiah, the Lord says to the Israelites, "For when I called, no one answered, when I spoke, no one listened."[203] It seems God had more vested interest in speaking to them than they had in listening to Him. The Israelites did not make hearing God a priority.

**Busyness** can be another obstruction to hearing God's voice. At a retreat once, I heard author and speaker Elisabeth Elliot say, "If Satan can't get you to sin, he'll keep you busy." We see this concept play out in Luke 10:38–42, which shines a light on the contrast between being busy for the Lord and sitting still at His feet to listen to what He says. In this passage, Jesus comes to visit two sisters, Martha and Mary. "Martha was distracted by all the preparations that had to be made" while Mary just "sat at the Lord's feet listening to what he said." So Martha complains to Jesus and asks Him to tell her sister to help her. Jesus replies with this: "Mary has chosen what is better, and it will not be taken away from her."

Jesus's reply shows us that even busyness in valuable endeavors, like family or ministry, can keep us from hearing His voice. In fact, I experienced this firsthand. For a time, out of shame and low self-worth, my identity became rooted in ministry. I was ministering from the wrong motive of wanting to earn God's approval — it was more about how much I did for God than about who I am as His daughter — and my busyness in serving God out of duty kept me from hearing His voice.

## Sin as an Obstacle to Hearing God

**Sin** is the all-encompassing stumbling block to clearly hearing the voice of the Lord, because sin separates us from God and hardens our hearts, which desensitizes our desire and ability to hear Him. There are various types of sin, of course, but here, I will touch upon a few types that I feel especially impede our ability to hear the Father's voice: unbelief, unforgiveness, fear of man, disobedience, and a rebellious heart.

**Unbelief** can be a major obstacle to hearing God's voice. Each step of our walk with God, beginning with salvation and going through sanctification, requires faith. We need faith in order to believe that the impressions we're having, the visions we're seeing, and the still, small voice we're hearing in our thoughts are actually from God. We must expect and anticipate that God not only wants to speak to us but that He *will* speak to us. When I struggle with doubt, I pray, "I do believe; help me overcome my unbelief!"[204]

Keeping **unforgiveness** in our hearts when we're wounded also gets in the way of hearing God's voice. When we harbor our wounds instead of freeing ourselves from them by forgiving our offender, we will have difficulty seeing or hearing things accurately, and this includes God's voice:

> Anyone who claims to be in the light but hates a brother or
> sister is still in the darkness. Anyone who loves his brother
> and sister lives in the light, and there is nothing in them to
> make them stumble. But anyone who hates a brother or sister
> is in the darkness and walks around in the darkness. They
> do not know where they are going, because the darkness has
> blinded him.[205]

Another way to think about this is that when we've been hurt by others and do not forgive them, we open the door to our own deception. When we're deceived, we can't see clearly; our perception is distorted and thus our interpretation of what's going on is off base. It's as if we're wearing the wrong prescription eyeglasses. It reminds me of one night when we had friends over for dinner. At one point I put on my glasses, and everything became blurry. Fearing I was having a stroke, I said, "John, John, I can't see!" At that moment, I realized I had mistakenly put on our friend's eyeglasses! Likewise, if we try to perceive God's voice through the wrong lenses of woundedness, the picture will come out fuzzy and we will be more likely to be deceived by what's in front of our noses. To accurately make out God's voice and His picture of things, we must put on His prescription lenses of forgiveness and a heart free of woundedness.

In my own life, **fear of man** has been a major stumbling block to hearing and obeying God's voice. In one instance I struggled with, I had a phone conversation with my mom. She happened to mention that she had never had her own doll. I knew she had lived in poverty as a little girl, but my heart was gripped with sadness when I learned she had never owned a doll. One morning, six weeks before Christmas, while spending time with the Lord, the Holy Spirit said, *"I want you to get your mom a doll for Christmas."*

I sat there, going back and forth talking with God, trying to get Him to understand why I couldn't do it. "But my dad would think I'm silly! After all, she's fifty-nine years old!" I eventually gave in and told Him I would obey, but I added that it would be nice if He could confirm in some way that this is what I was supposed to do — not necessary, but nice. Soon after, I went to Sam's Club and bought her a brunette porcelain doll. I wrapped it up and mailed it to her.

Then the week before Christmas, my four-year-old son and I were out running errands. In between stops, we were in the car, and he fell asleep, so I stopped the Psalty cassette tape we were listening to and turned the radio onto the Minirth-Meier counseling program. They were having a special call-in show, where people would telephone to share their most memorable Christmases. One man called in to share about when his fifty-nine-year-old mom had received her first doll. He said that she had embraced the doll and wept. I sobbed while driving down Industrial Road in Omaha! How kind of the Lord to give me such an undeniable confirmation when He didn't have to.

**Disobedience** is another form of sin that blocks our ability to hear God's voice. The Bible instructs us as follows: "Do not merely listen to the word, and so deceive yourselves. Do what it says."[206] Priscilla Shirer, in *Discerning the Voice of God*, writes, "God doesn't just speak to be heard. He speaks to be obeyed." In other words, if we're not planning on obeying God, we don't need to spend our time sitting still to listen. If we are listening for Him, we must be willing to follow Him.[207]

Think about it this way: If you asked an employee to do a task, and they didn't follow through, would you trust them enough to ask them next time you needed something done? What if the opposite were true, and they followed through instantly and completely? I think God is more apt to trust us when we consistently obey Him, and accordingly, He will speak to us more often.

Consider Jeremiah 42:1–22, when the Israelites asked the prophet Jeremiah to find out what God wanted them to do. They told him that whatever it was, they would be obedient. But in the end, they didn't comply with what God had asked of them. Commenting on this passage, Matthew Henry draws the following conclusion: "We do not truly desire to know the mind of God if we do not fully resolve to comply with it when we do know it."

That said, I sometimes still wrestle with obeying God. One time, the emcee at our church's simulcast missions conference encouraged people to come forward to the altar. Initially no one went forward. Then I heard the Spirit urging me, saying, *"Come."* I stayed seated. Even after hearing Him say "come" a few times, I stayed in my seat. I didn't understand why God would want me to go to the altar. After all, I wasn't experiencing any specific conviction or move on my heart.

The next morning, I heard God speak these words to me: *"Even if you're the only one Norma, even if you're all alone, if I say, 'Come,' I want you to do just that. Faint whispers, repeated commands, are all for your benefit — for your good and for my glory. You have no idea what you missed by disobeying me. Yes, even though you didn't 'feel' anything, any step toward surrender releases more of me."* I immediately repented.

If you haven't heard God's voice for a while, go back to the last thing He asked you to do. Did you do it? If not, repent and do it now, if it's not too late.

Lastly, **a rebellious heart** that does not want to be accountable to anyone thwarts our ability to hear God's voice. We won't hear God speak if that's our overriding heart attitude.

> Which of the above roadblocks have prevented you from hearing the Lord, either in the past or now? If you haven't ever heard God's voice, ask Him what is keeping you from hearing.

## Positioning Ourselves to Hear

*Here I am; you called me.*

1 SAMUEL 3:6B

Fortunately, we can overcome obstacles and posture ourselves to listen to the Lord by cultivating certain heart attitudes and taking a few practical steps.

### Heart Attitudes

If you can take a few minutes to read 1 Samuel 3:1–10, you will find that Samuel possessed several of the needed heart attitudes to hear God speak. When the Lord called Samuel, he immediately went to Eli, thinking it was Eli's voice and said, "Here I am; you called me." After this happened three times, Eli realized the Lord had called Samuel's name. So Eli instructed Samuel to say, "Speak, Lord, for your servant is listening." That is exactly what Samuel did. And when God spoke, Samuel responded with "Here I am."

This is also to be our response when God speaks to us. "Here I am" is an indication that we're present and near to Jesus; that we're available and allow God access to our hearts; and that we're willing to surrender to, serve, and immediately obey whatever God may call us to do. Like Samuel's, our heart attitude must be one of humility, dependence upon the Lord, and submission to God.

Another heart attitude of those who hear God speak is **childlike faith.** We see this in Matthew 11:25, when Jesus says, "I praise you, Father, Lord of heaven and earth, because you have hidden these things from the wise and learned, and revealed them to little children."[208] Children who have not been deliberately hurt or deceived by their parents will trust them to provide for their needs; it doesn't even enter their minds that their parents *won't* do this. Similarly, when we have childlike faith, we believe God wants to speak to us and trust that what He has to say is for our good. We don't ever doubt that we'll hear His voice.

In addition, hearing God's voice is unexplainable. It's not something you can rationally or intellectually understand; therefore, it takes simple, unadulterated, childlike faith to hear it.

We must also have **purity of heart** to hear God. Psalm 24:3–4a says, "Who may ascend the mountain of the Lord? Who may stand in His holy place? The one who has clean hands and a pure heart." Likewise, Matthew 5:8 says, "Blessed are the pure in heart, for they will see God." Being an unclogged vessel, free of sin, assists us to hear God speak. So don't be afraid of repentance. Shame will try to prevent you from repenting, but if you let it, it will also block your ability to hear God's voice. On the other hand, simply repenting will allow your friendship with God to be restored so that you can hear Him speak. Repentance is God's gift to us.

Having **a reverent and obedient heart** also opens a clear pathway to hearing God's voice. In the previous section, we looked at how disobedience can be an obstacle to hearing God, but disobedience isn't limited only to behavior; just like other behaviors, obedience begins as an attitude in our hearts. In 1 Samuel 15:22, we hear Samuel say this: "Does the Lord delight in burnt offerings and sacrifices as much as in obeying the Lord? To obey is better than sacrifice, and to heed is better than the fat of rams.'" In God's language, you spell *love* o-b-e-d-i-e-n-c-e. A heart that is willing to obey is necessary because, as we've seen, one of the most difficult parts about hearing God's voice is responding to what He says — trusting it and being obedient to it, especially when that requires taking risks and stepping out of our comfort zone.

Finally, **willingness** to hear and obey is an important heart condition in which our inner self is constantly positioned to hear God's voice. The Lord encouraged me with these words in 2015: *I will speak to you when you least expect it, my daughter. You don't have to be ready to listen (physically positioned* *to hear) as much as willing to listen so you can obey.* This willingness is a posture that our hearts take, wherever we go; it's as if we always have one ear cocked, leaning into God, and listening to the Spirit's voice.

> Describe a time when you heard and obeyed God's voice. What aspect of God did you discover? (Who was He to you in that experience?)

Finally, just as *not* prioritizing the Lord and his voice will prevent us from hearing God speak, desiring to **make Him and His words our top priority** will open our hearts to hearing Him more often. In 2014, God said to me, "*I go with you wherever you go. It's your commitment and faithfulness to me that I want to bless. It doesn't matter what room you're in or where you want to sit to hear my voice. What matters most is that you make time with me a priority. And that's what love looks like. What I like is knowing you want to be with me. It's not a chore or a duty or a responsibility to check off on your 'to do' list. Your pursuit of me is what gives you great favor with my heart. Your preferring me causes me to want to prefer you.*"

God loves to be pursued, and if He sees even a hint that you're interested in hearing His voice, He'll speak. So be intentional with your time. Value listening to His voice and linger in His presence. Ask God, "What do You want to say to me?"

Do I hear God accurately one hundred percent of the time? No. Do I sometimes think He's said something, but it's really my desire, and I've heard what I wanted to hear? Am I periodically deceived because of unhealed hurts or unforgiveness toward someone? I'm sure at times, all are true. But what is important is that my heart is genuine and set on wanting to hear God's voice and to obey Him. What matters to God is that I'm constantly pursuing a more intimate relationship with Him through sitting still and listening to His voice. God delights in seeing my ears cocked to hear even His slightest whisper.

## Practical Steps

Just as you can put your inner self in a position to better hear God, you can also put outward practices into place that will make you more attuned to listen to His voice. The first step is to **practice sitting still**. In other words, just do it! Spend a few minutes with God each day, or as often as you can, just sitting and listening for His voice. Each time you do, consider adding one, some, or all of the following steps:

- Before you start, take authority to silence the enemy, in the name of Jesus. Tell the Lord you that you desire to hear Him speak and that you believe He will speak. Ask the Holy Spirit to purify your heart, and confess and repent of any known sin. Then thank Him that He wants to speak to you. Start by saying the following prayer, which touches upon all of these items: "Jesus, I come to You to hear your voice. Thank you for your desire to speak to me. Bring to mind the sins I need to repent of, so I may confess them, receive your forgiveness, and have my heart purified. I take authority over the enemy's schemes and silence his lies and distractions. In Jesus's name, amen."

- Have a journal or paper nearby. Write down any distracting thoughts that threaten to interrupt you.

- Don't be discouraged if you don't hear God's voice. I don't hear Him speak every time I sit quietly before him. Just sitting still and being with Him speaks volumes of your love for Him and gives Him great pleasure. Allow those times of silence to make you more desperate to hear His voice. I think of it like the time I returned home from a mission trip to Mozambique. My husband and I sat on the couch with all the lights out, except those on the Christmas tree. He had his arm around me, and we sat in the dark, not saying a word. We felt our profound closeness even in the silence. In the same way, sometimes God will say to me, *"Can we just sit quietly together and not say anything?"* Those can be some of the most intimate times together.

- When He does speak, record what He says to you in a journal. Sometimes, I title the entry later and add it to a "table of contents" in the first few pages of the journal, so I'm able to find it when needed.

- If you feel so led, declare what you've journaled out loud. Sometimes, I'll even print specific words that I feel God is giving me and declare them out loud. Whenever I verbally proclaim God's promises, I begin to believe them more firmly, and faith is released within my heart that the promise is true.

Listening to God is not an exact science. But as with anything in life, the more you practice, the easier it gets. And no matter the outcome — whether God speaks or not, whether you're distracted or not, or whether you feel anything or not — the time and energy you put into being still with God will always bring nourishment to your soul and the relationship in the long run. And that is the main goal.

It reminds me of the message I heard my Father say to me in 2016: *"Listen, my daughter. Always give ear to what I have to say. For my words are truly your bread of life, your nourishment and what gives you sustenance. Feed on me and you will be strong. Take time to be with me like you take time to eat meals. I alone can give you what your heart and spirit need. Seek me and you will find me and, in the midst, all your needs will be met through me."* Similarly, when Satan tempted Jesus in the wilderness, Jesus responded to the enemy with these words: "It is written: 'Man shall not live on bread alone, but on every word that comes from the mouth of God.'"[209]

 How can you better prepare yourself to hear God's voice?

## Guidelines for Discerning God's Voice

*Whether you turn to the right or to the left, your ears will hear a voice behind you, saying, "This is the way; walk in it."*

ISAIAH 30:21

The more we get to know God, the more clearly we can hear His voice. Therefore, one of the biggest ways we can discern whether it's God's voice or the enemy's we're hearing is to understand who God is. One of the primary ways to do this is through reading the Word. **God's voice will never contradict or go against the Word of God, or be inconsistent with God's character.**

For example, in Ephesians 4:2 and 32, we discover the characteristics that God wants us to model after Him: "Be completely humble and gentle; be patient, bearing with one another in love. Be kind and compassionate to one another, forgiving each other, just as in Christ God forgave you." This tells us that God is humble, gentle, patient, kind, compassionate, and forgiving; therefore, His voice will be humble, not proud; gentle, not harsh; patient, not demanding; kind, not forceful or manipulative; compassionate, not distant and uncaring; and forgiving, not vengeful. Another good example is in Galatians 5:22–23a: "But the fruit of the Spirit is love, joy, peace, forbearance, kindness, goodness, faithfulness, gentleness and self-control." If what you're hearing does not resemble the fruit of the Holy Spirit, it most likely is not coming from God.

A few more characteristics to note, which are supported by Scripture: His voice will be filled with love and encouragement, even when He's bringing up a sin issue in our life. God does not condemn; rather, it's often God's kindness that woos us to repentance. As the Lord speaks, He will confirm our identity as His beloved children just as He does in Scripture.

It's so critical to get to know your heavenly Daddy by spending time in His Word, because God is consistent and doesn't change, even over millennia: "He who is the Glory of Israel does not lie or change his mind; for he is not a human being, that he should change his mind."[210]

A second principle that guides me to know whether it's God's voice I've heard is **peace**. When a word is truly from God, there will be peace about it within our hearts. Priscilla Shirer, in *Discerning the Voice of God*, describes it this way: "The green light of ease and peace means go." And the Passion translation of Proverbs 1:33 confirms this: "But the one who always listens to me will live undisturbed in a heavenly peace. Free from fear, confident and courageous, you will rest unafraid and sheltered from the storms of life."

It's important to note, however, that even though you may have peace about God's words, you may not always have peace about obeying those words. That is, if He's asked you to do something, you may be fearful to obey, but there is still peace that comes from a certain "knowing" that the words were from God. This is exactly how I felt when God asked my husband and me to go to Afghanistan. I knew without a doubt that God wanted us to go on this short-term mission trip, and in that sense, I had peace. But because the Taliban was still bombing the city of Kabul in hopes of taking it over, I remained fearful until the week before our trip, when one of our pastors prayed for me against the spirit of fear.

Another general rule in discerning God's voice is in regard to receiving **agreement or confirmation** of what God has spoken. In other words, God will sometimes give you prophetic words from others to confirm what you've been hearing. As Proverbs tells us, "In the Lord's hand, the king's heart is a stream of water that he channels toward all who please him."[211]

If you're single, you can ask a godly mentor, your pastor, a trustworthy Christian friend, or a Christian counselor for confirmation. If you're married and God is asking you to do something, your spouse will also give you a green light. It doesn't matter if your spouse knows or is walking closely with the Lord; if God is in the word, He can get your spouse's heart to give consent. Trust me — I know from personal experience that it is not worth doing something that you and your spouse do not see eye to eye on. Oneness with your spouse is a priority in God's economy.

Finally, in regard to feeling led to do something, when in doubt, don't! Or wait and keep praying for discernment. At the very least, run it by others who have a more mature walk with God and get their take on the word you've received. And ask God for confirmation.

There are good things in life to do and then there are God things. Wait for the ones God highlights to you.

> Which of these guidelines have you used to help you discern God's voice?

Finally, be aware that when God speaks to request something of you, His voice often takes on the following characteristics.

- **It takes you by surprise and is out in left field.** If you need to, ask for clarity and confirmation.

- **It's bigger than you, and you have to step out in faith to accomplish it.** In other words, you realize you can't do it in your own power. An example of this in my life was God's word to me to *"mentor the masses."* If this word is fulfilled, it will be because of God's ability, not mine. All I can give Him is my "yes," my availability. God will have to do the rest.

- **It's out of your comfort zone.** When God speaks, He frequently asks me to do things I would never do, or even consider doing, on my own.

God often asks us to put ourselves in positions out of our comfort zone so that we have to depend on Him to come through for us. This enables God to display His faithfulness to us and to manifest His power by "flexing His muscles" on our behalf. And when we follow through, it enables our faith to grow.

Learning to listen to God's voice reminds me of a hike that my husband and I went on with our Trek cycling tour group. John and I were among the oldest in the group, so we ended up in the back of the pack. Huffing and puffing, I wanted to give up after the first few uphill steps. It was too hard. I was tempted to tell the guide that I just wanted to turn around and go back to the hotel. Instead, I walked slowly and took frequent breaks to slow my heart rate. More than an hour later, we made it above the tree line. Ten majestic mountain peaks surrounded us in a stunning panorama. Rewarded with the view, I was so glad I had persevered.

In the same way, making it a priority to sit still with the Lord may be difficult at first and require some sacrifice, but let me tell you, hearing God's voice and deepening your intimacy with Him is always worth it. So I encourage you to step out of your comfort zone, establish a lifestyle of listening to the Father's voice, and make it a habit to obey. You won't be disappointed!

Put into practice what you've learned. Sit quietly before the Lord and see what happens.

. . . . . . . . . . . . . . . . . . . . . . . .

## What I Heard My Father Say

*My child, some of the most difficult things we do reap the biggest harvest. Listening to my voice is one of those things. The cost is your time, devotion, and attention, but the rewards are great. Chief among those rewards is greater attachment to me, which deepens our intimacy. There is so much I want to say to you! Would you sit still, spend time alone with me, and treasure our moments together?*

**Take time to wait before the Lord.**
**Ask Him what He wants to say to you regarding this chapter.**

## ~ The Heart of the Matter ~

- All relationships are built and deepened by communication.
- People hear God's voice more than they realize.
- God speaks when He knows we're willing to listen and obey.
- Listening to God's voice is a learning process.
- The more we know God, the more we'll trust Him. The more we trust Him, the more intimate we'll be.
- God will speak to us more often and be more apt to trust us when we consistently obey Him.
- We should not ask for a fresh word from God until we've obeyed the last one He gave.
- Possessing certain heart attitudes prepares us to listen to the Lord speak.
- Even if God is silent, sitting still and being in God's presence speaks volumes of our love for Him.
- A word from the Lord will never contradict or go against the Word of God. It also will not be inconsistent with God's character.
- When in doubt, don't! Or wait and keep praying for discernment.

# CONCLUSION

You did it! You persevered to the end. And you now probably know more about me than you want to! In seriousness, though, I pray that my stories of emotional healing resonated within your heart, shedding light on the principles and helping you to transform your life and intimacy with God.

One particular thread that I hope you take with you, woven throughout my experiences and this book alike, is found in Roman 8:28: "And we know that in all things God works for the good of those who love him, who have been called according to his purpose." This has been my life verse since I became a new believer at age fifteen, and it has stood the test of time. It speaks about God as the God of redemption, who weaves all of our experiences — the good, the bad, and the ugly — into a beautiful tapestry. By applying the principles in this book to your life, I hope you personally experience this verse's timeless truth, seeing firsthand that God works all things together for your good and His glory.

A second truth I hope you leave with is that I desire for all people to experience emotional wholeness, because there's just nothing like the taste of freedom; however, heart healing is not the end-all, be-all. In and of itself, emotional freedom has little meaning unless it propels us into the arms of Jesus, the One who died for our spiritual, mental, and emotional liberty and made those freedoms possible in the first place. So it is God who I hope you have a better picture of through reading this book. I pray you gain a greater understanding of who God is and how He works, of His presence and involvement in your life, and of how much He loves and accepts you.

And I especially hope you have come to know Him as *Baal Perazim*, "the God of the breakthrough," for He is the one who sets us free. Psalm 40:3 (TPT) says God does this for the purpose of others' amazement, so that they too can become intimate with Him: "A new song for a new day rises up in me every time I think about how he breaks through for me! Ecstatic praise pours out of my mouth until everyone hears how God has set me free. Many will see His miracles; they'll stand in awe of God and fall in love with him!"

So freedom is a gift that keeps on giving — and Jesus alone paid for this, so He alone is worthy of our wholehearted devotion. *Jesus* is the end-all, be-all.

In this vein, the final truth I hope you take with you is that Jesus wishes to partner with you on your healing journey as He did with the paralytic in John 5. So I pray that as you continue on your journey into deeper emotional wholeness, you will continue to fall more and more madly in love with Him.

Thanks for reading! If you loved the book and have a moment to spare, I would really appreciate a short review on Amazon, as this helps new readers find my book.

If this book has ministered to you, feel free to visit my website:
www.restoring-hearts.com
to learn more.

# ACKNOWLEDGMENTS

There's something very special and humbling when your family and friends believe in you, in God's destiny for your life, and, specifically, in your book project. I imagine it might be a little like what David, the shepherd-boy-turned-king, experienced in 1 Chronicles 11. David's mighty men rallied around him and gave him the support he needed to get where God wanted him to go. Likewise, the love and devotion of my "mighty men and women" have helped this part of my destiny come to fruition.

I'd especially like to thank my beloved husband, John. Thank you for believing in God's call on my life to write this book, for providing never-ending encouragement, and for continuing to help me with my noun-verb agreement!

To my children, Lindsay and David, and to David's fiancé, Kelsey — I have no greater delight than to spend time with you all and your dad! Lindsay, your beautiful artwork on the front cover, titled "Brave Heart," reminds me of the courageous woman that you are. David, the words you spoke to me more than twenty years ago while shopping at Barnes and Noble — "Mom, one day your picture and name will be up on this wall!" — still encourages my heart today.

To Mom, my stepdad Doug, and my dad in heaven, thank you for being my cheerleaders!

I have the utmost appreciation for Marylee Vecchio, the prayer coordinator for the Restoring Hearts Ministry prayer team. You have led the team well! Without these intercessors, and without the Omaha moms' prayer group and my Tuesday morning prayer group of three in Wichita, this book would still be only a dream.

To the men and women who piloted this book — your feedback has been invaluable. Thank you for making this a much better book than it originally was! When I reflect back on the first draft the women combed through, I am tempted to be embarrassed! You all not only critiqued but also encouraged me and extended grace.

Matthew and Angie Penner — you are quite the accountability team! Thank you for our brainstorming sessions, for asking me all the right questions to get me where I needed to be, and for gently holding me accountable. Angie, I treasure your servant's heart. Thank you for your foresight and for formatting the material to make it readable.

Charity Schaulis, you cheered me on to the finish line of the first draft of this book during my life-coaching sessions with you.

Staci Borgelt, I have great admiration for your eye for design and your gift of creativity to make the cover appealing to the eye.

Thanks also to Rick Waymire, of Body Life Ministries, who first published my writing material and continues to challenge me with a bigger vision.

A heartfelt thanks goes to Barb Shaw, who came alongside me with supportive scriptures for this book.

I especially treasure those on the Restoring Hearts Ministry board of directors, past and present, who have put their faith in this book project. You all helped get this ball rolling!

To the Wordsower's Christian Writers' Group in Omaha and the Tiny Tribe of Writers in Wichita, your friendship, instruction, guidance, and encouragement kept me going!

To my editor, Lynn Everett, thank you for making me sound so much better! You are a gift and an answer to prayer!

I appreciate Jenny Schwager's attention to the tiniest detail. I'm grateful for your proofreading skills.

Thank you to those who took the time to be the first readers of this book and to write endorsements. I value your stamp of approval.

And to Jesus, the Lover of my soul, thank you for inviting me into intimacy with you through the writing of this book. I am more deeply in love with you as a result.

# ABOUT THE AUTHOR

NORMA DONOVAN is an author, speaker, and the founder and president of Restoring Hearts Ministry. With a master's degree in counseling, her passions include mentoring women, being intimate with God, and seeing others' hearts restored.

Norma and her husband live in Kansas, and have two grown children.

# TOPICAL BIBLIOGRAPHY

## Attachment

Clinton, Tim and Gary Sibcy. *Attachments: Why You Love, Feel, and Act the Way You Do.* Brentwood, TN: Integrity, 2002.

Cloud, Henry. *Changes that Heal: How to Understand Your Past to Ensure a Healthier Future.* Grand Rapids, MI: Zondervan, 1992.

## Emotional Healing

Fresh Start. *Processing the Issues of Your Heart.* www.freshstartforallnations.org. This website is full of other resources on emotional healing as well.

Gardner, Thom. *Healing the Wounded Heart: Removing Obstacles to Intimacy with God.* Shippensburg, PA: Destiny Image, 2005.

Thompson, Curt. *Anatomy of the Soul: Surprising Connections between Neuroscience and Spiritual Practices that Can Transform Your Life and Relationships.* Carol Stream, IL: Tyndale, 2010.

## Fear

Joyner, Rick. *Overcoming Fear.* Wilkesboro, NC: MorningStar, 2002.

## Forgiveness

Fresh Start. *Processing the Issues of Your Heart.* www.freshstartforallnations.org. This ministry's vision is to see people become free through the transforming power of forgiveness in Jesus Christ.

Marshall, Tom. *Right Relationships: How to Create Them & How to Restore Them.* Kent, TN: Sovereign World, 1992.

Stoop, David. *Forgiving the Unforgivable.* Ventura, CA: Gospel Light, 2003.

Stoop, David. *Making Peace with Your Father.* Wheaton, IL: Tyndale House, 1992.

## Hearing God's Voice

Dawson, Joy. *Forever Ruined for the Ordinary: The Adventure of Hearing and Obeying God's Voice.* Nashville, TN: Thomas Nelson, 2001.

Meyer, Joyce. *How to Hear from God: Learn to Know His Voice and Make Right Decisions.* New York, NY: Warner Faith, 2003.

Shirer, Priscilla. *Discerning the Voice of God: How to Recognize When God is Speaking.* Chicago, IL: Moody, 2007.

Stanley, Charles. *How to Listen to God.* Nashville, TN: Thomas Nelson, 1985.

## Identity in Christ

Anderson, Neil. *Victory over the Darkness: Realizing the Power of your Identity in Christ.* Ventura, CA: Gospel Light, 1990.

Bown, Allison. *The Image: Experience Your Life from God's Perspective.* Vancouver, WA: Brilliant Book House, 2018.

Frost, Jack. *Spiritual Slavery to Spiritual Sonship: Your Destiny Awaits You.* Shippensburg, PA: Destiny Image, 2006.

Smeltzer, Kristen. *Who Do You Say I Am? Overcoming the Spirit of Identity Theft.* N.p.: Destiny Oak, 2017.

## Intimacy with Christ

Chan, Francis. *Crazy Love: Overwhelmed by a Relentless God.* Colorado Springs, CO: David C. Cook, 2008.

Guyon, Jeanne. *Intimacy with Christ.* Jacksonville, FL: SeedSowers, 2001.

Taylor, Wade. *The Secret of the Stairs: A Guide to Spiritual Growth from the Song of Solomon.* Hagerstown, MD: McDougal, 1988.

Tozer, A. W. *The Pursuit of God: The Human Thirst for the Divine.* Camp Hill, PA: Wing Spread, 1982.

Wright, Alan. *Lover of My Soul: Delighting in God's Passionate Love.* Sisters, OR: Multnomah, 1998.

## Knowing God

Packer, J. I. *Knowing God.* Downers Grove, IL: InterVarsity, 1973.

Pink, Arthur. *The Attributes of God.* Grand Rapids, MI: Baker, 1975.

## Rejection

Meyer, Joyce. *Approval Addiction: Overcoming Your Need to Please Everyone.* New York, NY: Warner Faith, 2005.

Jackson, John Paul. *Breaking Free of Rejection.* North Sutton, NH: Streams, 2004.

Prince, Derek. *God's Remedy for Rejection.* New Kensington, PA: Whitaker House, 1993.

Sorge, Bob. *Dealing with the Rejection and Praise of Man.* Greenwood, MO: Oasis House, 1999.

## Renewing Your Mind

Anderson, Neil. *The Bondage Breaker: Overcoming Negative Thoughts, Irrational Feelings, Habitual Sins.* Eugene, OR: Harvest House, 1990.

Backus, William and Marie Chapian. *Telling Yourself the Truth: Find Your Way out of Depression, Anxiety, Fear, Anger, and Other Common Problems by Applying the Principles of Misbelief Therapy.* Minneapolis, MN: Bethany Fellowship, 1980.

Meyer, Joyce. *Battlefield of the Mind: Winning the Battle in Your Mind.* Tulsa, OK: Harrison House, 1995.

Thurman, Chris. *The Lies We Believe: Learn to Replace These Lies with the Truth and Discover the Happiness You've Been Seeking.* Nashville, TN: Thomas Nelson, 1989.

## Shame

Humbert, Cynthia Spell. *Deceived by Shame, Desired by God.* Colorado Springs, CO: Navpress, 2001.

Malone, Henry. *Shame: Identity Thief.* Irving, TX: Vision Life, 2006.

Powers, Marie. *Shame: Thief of Intimacy.* Ventura, CA: Gospel Light, 1998.

Smedes, Lewis. *Shame and Grace: Healing the Shame We Don't Deserve.* New York, NY: HarperCollins, 1993.

Wilson, Sandra. *Released from Shame: Moving beyond the Pain of the Past.* Downers Grove, IL: InterVarsity, 1990.

Wright, Alan. *Shame Off You: Washing Away the Mud that Hides Our True Selves.* Sisters, OR: Multnomah, 2005.

# NOTES

1   John 5:6

2   Psalm 121:4

3   See Matthew 10:30

4   Matthew 6:8b

5   Philippians 4:19 (emphasis mine)

6   See Psalm 100:3, Isaiah 43:1–2, and 1 John 4:4, 6

7   See Hebrews 13:5 and John 14:26 (NIV)

8   See 1 Peter 5:7b

9   See 1 Thessalonians 2:4; Ephesians 1:6 (KJV)

10  See Ephesians 2:10 and Psalm 138:8 (ESV)

11  See Romans 5:8, 1 John 4:10, and Jeremiah 31:3

12  See John 3:16 and Ephesians 2:8–9

13  See Zephaniah 3:17

14  Mark 10:16

15  See 2 Corinthians 1:3

16  Isaiah 66:13

17  Matthew 22:37–39

18  Hebrews 12:10b-11

19  Revelation 19:11–16

20  John 10:11b

21  Matthew 1:21b

22  See Isaiah 48:17

23  Matthew 5–7

24  Luke 10:38–42

25  See Psalm 62:8

26  See Romans 2:4

27  See Luke 4:14–30

28  See John 7:1–5

29  See Matthew 26:69–75

30  See Genesis 4:2b-8

31  See Genesis 16:3–14

32  1 Peter 2:23

33  1 Peter 4:19

34  See Proverbs 29:25

35  See Ephesians 4:15

36  See Philippians 3:3

37  Galatians 1:10

38  Luke 3:22

39  See Psalm 142:4

40  See John 10:10

41  See John 3:16

42  See 2 Corinthians 5:21

43  See John 17:23

44  See John 1:12

45  See Ephesians 1:6

46  See 1 Peter 2:9

47  See Ephesians 1:5

48  See Romans 8:17

49  See Colossians 2:10

50  See Psalm 149:4 (NKJV)

51  Genesis 50:20

52  See Romans 8:29

53  See Genesis 3:8

54  Jonah 2:8

55  1 John 1:9

56  See Romans 2:4

57  Psalm 51:10a

58  Psalm 51:4a

59  Matthew 6:14–15

60  1 Peter 2:23

61  Colossians 3:13

62  Luke 6:28

63  See Psalm 34:18

64  Psalm 62:8

65  Psalms 142:1–2

66  Isaiah 61:7

67  See Numbers 13:27

68  See Numbers 13:31–14:4

69  See Numbers 14:5–9

70  See Numbers 14:23 and Hebrews 3:19

71  Matthew 8:26

72  Philippians 4:13

73  Mark 9:24

74  Galatians 6:7–8

75  See Romans 8:5–7

76  Philippians 4:13

77  Matthew 7:1–2

78  See Genesis 3:1–5

79  John 14:6 (emphasis mine)

80  See John 3:17–18a

81  Romans 2:4b; John 16:8

82  Revelation 12:10b

83  John 8:32

84  1 John 1:9

85  See 1 John 1:9

86  See 2 Corinthians 10:4–5

87  Ephesians 1:6 and 1 Peter 2:9

88  1 Corinthians 15:57

89  John 3:16

90  1 Corinthians 2:16

91  Philippians 4:13

92  Colossians 1:14

93  Romans 10:17

94  See Matthew 4:1–11

95  Job 42:5

96  Luke 15:29

97  Genesis 3:16

98  See Romans 8:28

99  See Psalm 103:13

100  See Luke 5:20

101  See Psalm 139

102  Psalm 18:2

103  See Malachi 3:6

104  See Deuteronomy 7:9

105  2 Chronicles 20:15b

106  Isaiah 40:10a

107  See Isaiah 62:5

108  Song of Solomon 2:10b, 13b

109  See Hosea 2:16

110  John 14:26

111  See John 16:8

112  John 16:13

113  Romans 2:4b

114  Matthew 11:6 ESV

115  See 2 Corinthians 7:10

116  Exodus 20:3

117  See Deuteronomy 32:19

118  See Deuteronomy 13:6–11

119  See Isaiah 2:9

120  See Isaiah 44:17

121  Habakkuk 2:18

122  See Habakkuk 2:18

123  See Deuteronomy 32:18

124  See Deuteronomy 32:20b

125  See Psalm 97:7a

126  See Deuteronomy 4:28

127  See Isaiah 46:7b

128  See Isaiah 44:9–10 and Jeremiah 2:11b

129  See Jeremiah 10:5b

130    See Psalm 115:4–8 and 135:15–18

131    See Jeremiah 10:6

132    See Jeremiah 10:10

133    See Proverbs 18:10

134    See Isaiah 46:10–11

135    See Jeremiah 2:13b

136    See 1 Corinthians 10:14

137    See Exodus 34:13

138    See 2 Chronicles 5:13–14

139    Philippians 2:8

140    Luke 3:21–22

141    Genesis 22:2

142    Luke 22:42

143    Philippians 2:8b

144    James 4:17

145    I Samuel 15:26

146    Deuteronomy 28:1–14; 30:1–10

147    Deuteronomy 10:12–13 (emphasis mine)

148    Deuteronomy 5:33, Isaiah 1:19, Luke 5:1–7

149    See Matthew 25:14–30

150    See Genesis 37:2–50:26 (Joseph's life)

151    See Job 22:21 & 36:11, Psalm 119:165, Jeremiah 6:16, and Romans 8:29

152    See Genesis 12:1–3, and The Book of Esther

153    2 Corinthians 9:13

154    Deuteronomy 28:15–68

155    Jonah 1:1–2:10

156    John 2:5b

157    Romans 4:17

158    Exodus 3:11

159    See Psalm 45:11

160    See Ephesians 4:7

161    See 1 Peter 2:9

162    See Luke 12:7

163    See Ephesians 2:8–9, Colossians 1:22, and 1 Corinthians 1:8

164    See Isaiah 62:4–5 and Zephaniah 3:17

165    See Romans 5:8

166    See Psalm 118:6

167    Psalm 103:12

168    Psalm 139:14

169    2 Corinthians 10:12

170    1 John 4:18

171    Luke 15:29 (emphasis mine)

172    See John 1:12

173    See Ephesians 2:10

174    See Philippians 3:20 and Ephesians 2:6

175    See 2 Corinthians 5:17

176    See John 15:15

177    See Ephesians 4:24

178    See Colossians 3:12 and 1 Thessalonians 1:4

179    See Ephesians 1:1

180    See Genesis 3:8

181    Exodus 24:15–16

182    See Exodus 33:7

183    See Exodus 33:11

184    Philippians 3:10

185    See Exodus 33:18

186    See Exodus 33:19

187    See Exodus 33:20–23

188    See Exodus 33:16

189    See Genesis 32:22–32

190    See Mark 10:46–52

191    See 2 Samuel 6:14–22

192    See Mark 5:24–34

193    See Ephesians 3:17–19

194    Psalm 107:9

195    Psalm 23:1–3a

196   Exodus 33:14

197   Isaiah 30:21

198   Genesis 12:1

199   Jeremiah 33:3

200   See Matthew 2:13

201   See Matthew 2:19–20

202   See Nehemiah 7:5

203   Isaiah 66:4b

204   Mark 9:24b

205   1 John 2:9–11

206   James 1:22

207   See John 10:27

208   Matthew 11:25

209   Matthew 4:4

210   1 Samuel 15:29

211   Proverbs 21:1

*www.restoring-hearts.com*

Made in the USA
Monee, IL
02 March 2021

61757730R10122